MAY ALCOTT

A Memoir

MAY ALCOTT
From the crayon portrait

MAY ALCOTT

A Memoir

By CAROLINE TICKNOR

WITH

ILLUSTRATIONS

APPLEWOOD BOOKS

CARLISLE, MASSACHUSETTS

May Alcott: A Memoir
was originally published in 1928.

ISBN 978-1-4290-9312-5

Thank you for purchasing an Applewood book.
Applewood reprints America's lively classics—
books from the past that are still of
interest to modern readers.
Our mission is to build a picture of the past
through primary sources.

To inquire about this edition
or to request a free copy
of our current print catalog
featuring our best-selling books, write to:
Applewood Books
P.O. Box 27
Carlisle, MA 01741
For more complete listings,
visit us on the web at:
www.awb.com

Manufactured in the United States of America

TO

My Sister

EDITH SLADE TICKNOR

this volume is affectionately dedicated

PREFACE

EVER since her first entry into the book world, "Amy the Artist" of "Little Women" has held her place as one of the most vivid creations in the field of fiction. A sparkling and appealing personality, who from the start won widespread popularity among the lovers of Louisa Alcott's books, she was so much alive that she provoked countless inquiries from interested readers, who begged for further information concerning her, until Miss Alcott's patience was well-nigh exhausted. And now, though sixty years have passed, "Amy" still holds her own among the best-beloved girl heroines.

Undoubtedly, the secret of her strong appeal lies not so much in the fact that her portrayal by her sister was absolutely true to life, as that it pictured one who was herself so vividly alive. May Alcott possessed a rare capacity for living and enjoying. She loved life, she loved beauty, she loved people; the world of nature and the world of art gave her the keenest pleasure; she loved to walk, run, row, and ride, reveled in strenuous exertion, and worked with tireless energy in the pursuit of her objectives. Unhampered by the heritage of that New England conscience which ruled Louisa with a rod of iron, she steered straight for the goal in the art world that from the first had fired her imagination, and her steadfast endeavors were rewarded with no small measure of success.

To those who know her only as Louisa Alcott's youngest sister, the following extracts from her correspondence and from her mother's journal should prove of interest as outlining more clearly the sisterly relationship and casting new light on a famous writer and her household; while to those readers who cherish a genuine affection for "Amy," her life-story will furnish the answer to the oft-formulated questions concerning the authentic history of the "artist" in "Little Women."

Her story is that of a happy life and of one gifted with that Golden Touch which transmits joy to all with whom it comes in contact. It is the story of an artist's work early cut off, but of an artist whose influence still lives in the development of the art-life in her own land, an end for which she strove with unabated zeal.

Her correspondence which remains is for the most part concerned with the description of her life as an art student in London and in Paris, where she made contacts with many famous personages and embryo painters destined for world-wide fame in after years. These letters present vivid pictures of the dramatic scenes surrounding the opening of the Salon in 1877, voicing her point of view as a successful applicant for admission to the great exhibition. Her earlier correspondence pictures her journeying through Europe with Louisa, when author and art student studied Old-World châteaux, which furnished one food for her pen, the other material for her brush, while her last letters tell the story of her romantic marriage and brief idyllic life in her new home in France. Interspersed with May's sprightly epistles are sympathetic extracts from Mrs. Alcott's journal, which still more fully aid in the interpretation of the lives of the gifted Alcott sisters and of their famous parents.

In the compilation of this memoir, thanks are due to Messrs. Little, Brown, and Company for their courtesy in supplying Alcott data from their various publications, and to Mrs. F. Alcott Pratt for her kindly coöperation in furnishing May Alcott's letters and extracts from Mrs. Alcott's journal; and also to Daniel Chester French, who for a brief time has laid aside his chisel in order to pay tribute with his pen to one who gave him his first lump of clay and sculptor's tools.

CONTENTS

ILLUSTRATIONS

ONE sparkling summer's morning in 1868 a young woman rode into our yard in Concord, Massachusetts, wearing the long skirt and close-fitting bodice which, with plumed hat, made up the picturesque riding habit of that day, setting off her tall and extraordinarily handsome figure to advantage. This was May Alcott. I recall that the impression she made on my mother was one of impatience, for the horse's hoofs sadly marred the lawn; but upon me the impression was one of abounding life and health and spirit which has stayed by me for more than half a century.

Her face was not beautiful, according to classical standards, but the liveliness of expression and the intelligence and gayety that shone from it led one to overlook any want of harmony in her features. She wore her wavy chestnut hair, luxuriant and glistening, like a crown, I thought. An intimate friend said of her, "If it were the fashion to go without clothes, May would be considered the most beautiful creature in the world."

Full of the joy of living, her enthusiasm was easily stirred in almost any worth-while direction, whether the matter in hand was the painting of a

[xv]

picture or the painting of a room in her house, or the getting up of a dance or a picnic on the river—forms of amusement prevalent in Concord in her time.

The home life of the Alcotts has been so vividly reflected in her gifted sister's books that it would be superfluous to describe it here. I must, however, refer to the spirit of happiness that pervaded it and the cordial hospitality which one always met there. May was fond of her home and a quite ideal relationship existed between her and her father and mother and sisters. She, more than the others, contributed to the lively and gay element in the household.

The house, set well back from the road over which the British marched on their famous visit to Concord in 1775, was a modest dwelling in a setting of elms and shrubbery. The low-ceilinged rooms were furnished very plainly with a mixture of styles resulting from many years of occupancy, but with evidence in pictures and books of the cultivation of the inmates. I once asked a distinguished architect what constituted homelikeness in a house. "Absence of architecture," he replied. The home of the Alcotts had this precious quality for which the "period room" strives in vain.

The impress of the artist member of the family was felt in the water colors, charcoals, and oil paintings which were the fruit of her studies with

William Hunt. A bust in plaster of "Mercury" which stood on a pedestal in the "front entry" attested to her course of study with Doctor Rimmer. Over the entrance door of the room which served as her studio was an inscription: "True genius is infinite patience. — Michael Angelo." My brother tried in vain to find this sentiment among Michael Angelo's recorded writings or sayings. Years afterwards a friend in talking with him said, "You know 'true genius is infinite patience'." He eagerly asked where she found the quotation. "In 'Little Women,'" said she. "Thus," as he said, "I had chased my quotation into the same hole it came out of." I wonder whether Michael Angelo or the philosophical Alcott originated the remark?

At the time of which I speak, I was a youth of eighteen or twenty. I was always included, however, in the frequent invitations to supper or evening gatherings where there were literary games or charades or only conversation. Serene and courtly, his long silver locks curling about his neck, his fresh pink and white complexion set off by an expanse of snowy linen, with white cravat, Mr. Alcott had much the aspect of an old portrait. He looked on at our diversions as from a loftier sphere, occasionally joining in the conversation or smiling approvingly at the humor of it, while

the dear old lady who had not only been his
helpmeet, but also a mainstay to the erratic genius
through the many anxious years before the talented
Louisa came so gallantly to the rescue, lent to the
occasion her sweet reasonableness and her ever-
quick response. The daughters, however, were
most in evidence, as their elders seemed to wish.
Miss Louisa's nimble wit and Miss May's gayety
were sure to make material for diversion. One
felt that here indeed "people were of more importance than things."

May was eminently social and far more fond of
society than her sisters. She entered into the quiet
social life of our town with zest, finding, however,
a wider field among her friends in Boston.

I have referred to her studies with Hunt and
Rimmer. Both of these talented artists contributed to her art education in ways as different as
the men themselves. Mr. Hunt had a class in
drawing and painting, conducted much like the
classes at the *École des Beaux Arts* in Paris. A
studio was provided where the students worked
from casts or still-life or living models, and which
was visited from time to time by the master,
whose studio was under the same roof. These
classes were exclusively for women. By special
dispensation, I was once granted the privilege of

joining the class, but I found, after attending once or twice, that I was an embarrassing circumstance and I therefore reluctantly withdrew and never went again. I have regretted this sacrifice ever since, as there was no other place in Boston at that time where a youth could find instruction in drawing. Here, however, May Alcott found the instruction and practice she needed and of which she made such good use. Hunt got his training in Paris and among the since famous Barbizon painters. He evidently was a good teacher, as all good painters are not; full of enthusiasm, which provoked a ready response in his pupils. They idolized him and made no secret of their idolatry.

Doctor Rimmer, with whom Miss Alcott studied not only drawing but modeling, also had a class composed mostly of young women. His teaching was chiefly of the figure and his method was eminently his own. Swiftly, but with surprising accuracy, he would make outline drawings on a blackboard, in the presence of his class, of parts or the whole of the human frame and these his pupils were required to copy. Meanwhile he discoursed most interestingly and instructively, and sometimes managed to convey to his proselytes a part at least of his profound knowledge of anatomy. He was a remarkable man and a gifted sculptor.

PRELUDE

That May Alcott's teachers did not in the least understand or appreciate each other was evident, nor did they attempt to conceal their opinions of each other's methods. "The trouble with Mr. Hunt is that he can't draw," said Doctor Rimmer to his class; while Mr. Hunt exclaimed, when I told him that I had drawn under Doctor Rimmer, "Oh, that stuff Rimmer does is n't drawing." They saw nature with different eyes, Doctor Rimmer chiefly interested in line; Mr. Hunt in masses of light and shade and color; yet both were great artists and May Alcott seems to have reconciled their conflicting methods in her own work.

I may be permitted to record the peculiar debt I owe her in introducing me to the potentialities of sculpture. I had been whittling and carving things from wood and gypsum, and even from turnips, as many boys do, and, as usual, "the family" thought the product remarkable. My father spoke about them to Miss Alcott, as the artist of the community, and she, with her ever-ready enthusiasm, immediately offered to give me her modeling clay and tools. I lost no time in harnessing the horse and driving over for them, and in experimenting with the seductive material, although I did n't know even how to moisten it. I still have one of the modeling tools she gave me.

PRELUDE

While I know of some misguided people who will not consider that she is to be commended for this service to me, *I* am constantly grateful.

Miss Alcott went abroad in 1870 with her sister Louisa, and again in 1873 and 1876 alone. She pursued her art studies in Paris and in London, where she was particularly impressed by Turner's paintings. She made copies of a number of them and her success may be judged by the fact that she won the attention of Ruskin. This great critic and admirer of Turner pronounced them the best reproductions of Turner's works that had ever been done.

It was during her third visit abroad that she met Ernest Nieriker. This young Swiss sympathized with her artistic ambitions and appreciated the promise of her gifts. They were married in 1878, but their happiness was brief, since she died a year later, leaving him with a little daughter.

Miss Alcott was devoted to her art and gave to it the best of her enthusiastic nature. She had talent and training, and her works, particularly her water colors, have a very distinct charm. Her sketches are still eagerly sought, both for their intrinsic value and for their association with the name of Alcott.

DANIEL CHESTER FRENCH

GLENDALE, MASSACHUSETTS,
June 14, 1926

MAY ALCOTT

A Memoir

IN THE GARRET

BY LOUISA M. ALCOTT

Four little chests all in a row,
Dim with dust, and worn by time,
All fashioned and filled, long ago,
By children now in their prime.
Four little keys hung side by side,
With faded ribbons, brave and gay,
When fastened there with childish pride,
Long ago, on a rainy day.
Four little names, one on each lid,
Carved out by a boyish hand,
And underneath, there lieth hid
Histories of the happy band
Once playing here, and pausing oft
To hear the sweet refrain,
That came and went on the roof aloft,
In the falling summer rain.

. . . .

Upon the last lid's polished field —
Legend now both fair and true —
A gallant knight bears on his shield,
"Amy," in letters gold and blue.
Within, the snoods that bound her hair,
Slippers that have danced their last,
Faded flowers laid by with care,
Fans whose airy toils are past —
Gay valentines all ardent flames,
Trifles that have borne their part
In girlish hopes, and fears, and shames.
The record of a maiden heart,
Now learning fairer truer spells,
Hearing, like a blithe refrain,
The silver sound of bridal bells
In the falling summer rain.

CHAPTER I

The Little May Queen

"A REGULAR snow maiden, with blue eyes, and yellow hair curling on her shoulders, pale and slender, and always carrying herself like a young lady mindful of her manners." In these lines Louisa Alcott flashes the searchlight upon her youngest sister, May, the "Amy" of "Little Women."

They called her "Little Raphael", for she early developed an intense love of beauty, and displayed a talent for drawing, which convinced them that she possessed unusual artistic gifts. From the first, she was regarded as the lucky child, the mascot of the family, on whom the others delighted to bestow pretty trifles, and who wielded the scepter accorded her, when as a baby she rode upon the shoulders of her sisters, crowned with flowers, their tiny "May" Queen.

Born in Concord, Massachusetts, on July 26, 1840, in the Hosmer cottage, described in "Little Women" as "Meg's first home", this youngest daughter, named after her mother Abba May (or Abigail May), came upon the scene shortly before the trying experiment at "Fruitlands", that pitiful Utopia where her father proved the fruitlessness of an attempt at too high thinking coupled with too plain living. From this parent, who throughout his life displayed much skill with pen and pencil, although little has been recorded concerning his talent in this direction, the youngest daughter undoubtedly inherited her artistic gift and various other traits; whereas her sister Louisa possessed her mother's characteristics to a great degree.

The early history of the Alcott family has been so fully chronicled elsewhere that a brief outline here seems all-sufficient.

Amos Bronson Alcott was born in 1799, on his father's farm, near Wolcott, Connecticut, where his early years were spent amid rural surroundings, yet, although his parents were hard-working farmer folk, they had behind them distinguished Anglo-Saxon stock, and Alcott counted a Lord Chancellor of England, and other prominent men, among his forbears, the name being spelled Alcocke in former times. Alcott's intense love of books and his desire for education were early manifested, and with small opportunities he prepared himself for the career that he desired, that of a teacher and philosopher.

THE LITTLE MAY QUEEN

In 1830, he married Abigail May, daughter of Colonel Joseph May, of Boston, whose mother, Dorothy Sewall, was a descendant of a family famed in the early annals of Massachusetts. She possessed the keen intellectual qualities of her ancestors, combined with great practical ability. She was a woman of fine physique, full of life and spirit, and her untiring energy was freely expended for the benefit of her family and those about her. Marriage with an idealist who had no faculty for money-making brought her many trials and privations, but she bore them cheerily and never wavered in her affection for her husband, or her devotion to her children.

Of the four "Little Women" — "Meg", "Jo", "Beth", and "Amy" — only the youngest sister was a native of Concord. Anna and Louisa were born in Germantown, Pennsylvania, while Elizabeth, and a little brother, who died in infancy, were born in Boston.

May's birth, following close upon her father's grief at the loss of his infant son, and the failure of his school in Boston, seemed to usher in a new and brighter era for the family, which came with their removal from Boston to Concord; and Bronson Alcott wrote in his journal, in the summer of 1840, of this happy event:

[5]

"A new life has arrived to us (July 26). She was born with the dawn, and is a proud little Queen, not deigning to give us the light of her royal presence, but persists in sleeping all the time, without notice of the broad world of ourselves. Providence, it seems, decrees that we shall provide selectest ministries alone, and so sends us successive daughters of Love to quicken the Sons of Life. We joyfully acquiesce in the Divine behest and are content to rear women for the future world. As yet their ministry is unknown in the culture of the nations, but the hour draws near when love shall be felt as a chosen Bride for Wisdom, and the celestial pair preside over all the household of mankind."

The youngest child, who came with the sunrise, seemed made for love, sunshine, and happiness. And as she was at the first designated, so she continued to grow up, the little "Queen", whose qualities were enumerated on her first Christmas Eve by her father, who wrote: —

For Abba
1840
For Abba
Babe fair,
Pretty hair,

[6]

THE LITTLE MAY QUEEN

Bright eye,
Deep sigh,
Sweet lip,
Feet slip,
Handsome hand,
Stout grand,
Happy smile,
Time beguile,
All I ween,
Concordia's Queen.

Many details of family life during this period may be gleaned from the youthful diaries of the small sisters, who with their pens fulfilled one of their father's pet requirements. The keeping of a journal was viewed by Mr. Alcott as a most vital part of his theory of education, and for this, as well as for the art of letter-writing, he strove to kindle the enthusiasm of his children, setting them an example by numberless epistles written upon their birthdays, at Christmastide, and on innumerable occasions. And then, with utmost care, he patiently arranged, filed, and preserved all these productions, the earliest of which are from his eldest daughter's pen.

Anna began her journal at eight years and her example was followed by Louisa, and then by Elizabeth; while baby May, proving less amenable to educational precepts, was allowed to express her thoughts in the pictorial manner she had early chosen for her own.

Anna wrote in her journal in October, 1839:

"We spend an hour or more every morning at our lessons with father, writing, reading, drawing, spelling, dephyning and talking. I have never been to any other school but father's: he has taught me most that I know about myself and other things. I do not know that I shall have any other teacher. . . . We read about Jesus walking on the water and Peter sinking in it. I like to read about Jesus, because he is so good. Father is the best man in the world now."

In November of the same year, she writes:

"I read some of the story of little Henri this morning while in bed. Father talked with us about Temperance at breakfast. I think I am temperate. I have few pains."

A few days later, on November 29th, a double birthday anniversary was celebrated, and Anna wrote:

"This is father's and Louisa's birthday. We gave them many presents; to father a portfolio for his papers, and a pocket pincushion. To Louisa, a box full of things, and a beautiful doll, with Letters from Father and Mother. She seems very happy playing with them, and we were all happy in making them for her; she is seven years old today, father is forty. I am eight and shall be nine if I live till the 15th of March next, and I hope to write a better journal than this."

In Anna's journal, which faithfully reflects her father's educational methods, the frequent references to "baby sister" enable one to picture the ten-year-old assuming the rôle of little mother to tiny May, and at the same time striving to live up to the moral standards, and to digest the "conversations" which formed the basis of Bronson Alcott's educational régime.

At the age of nine, Anna is learning to accept the gospel of "going without." She writes:

"Wednesday I spent the morning with father and sisters; he read to us and we read to him from the New Testament about unclean appetites and evil passions; he read about the Muck-Rake of Selfishness. Father told us how people had treated him, and why he came to Concord, and how we must give up a good many things that we like.

I know it will be hard, but I mean to do it. I fear I shall complain about it."

In 1834, Mr. Alcott had opened the "Temple School" in Boston, where he put into practice his educational ideas, which, however, proved too far ahead of his time to be appreciated. He made religion and character-building a vital part of his curriculum, and opened his sessions with instruction in manners and behavior, while his plan for punishing the unruly was a reversal of the custom of chastising a pupil; in place of the old method, Alcott insisted that the boy deserving punishment should administer several blows to his teacher in the presence of the school. This experiment when tried worked to a charm. Following a tearful refusal to strike the kind instructor, the pupil in question was forced to administer the punishment, a procedure which made so lasting an impression on all that from the time of its first application the ferrule was totally discarded. These innovations in the schoolroom, however, did not meet with the approval of those who resented any departure from the old-time methods, and the school proving a failure, the teacher, cheered by the thought of being near his loved friend Emerson, had turned his face towards Concord.

The idea of "giving up", which was so early instilled into the minds of the elder children, made less impression upon May, the baby of the family. And it was generally her portion to secure the gratification of her youthful wants, perhaps because she wanted things so much, and did not hesitate to voice her needs emphatically.

May's earliest attendance upon lessons is noted in Anna's journal, in September, 1840, when she writes:

"We had *baby* in the school, and she seemed almost to talk, she said 'coo, coo.' She is not quite six-weeks old."

If at this period May failed to profit by her father's teaching, her ten-year-old sister strove earnestly to do so, and wrote of those endeavors:

"My long lessons were right this morning and I was glad. I did not feel well and tended baby while father talked with Louisa about prayer. I do not call words prayer, but thoughts — feelings and resolution. . . . Our reading today was upon the New Testament about Jesus talking with the people and answering their hard questions. We read his Parable of the Husbandman and the Vineyard. I should like to talk with Jesus."

This early journal is full of suggestions about "tending baby" and having "useful talks" with her father, of whose instruction she says:

"I hope I shall govern myself and not need father and mother to govern me. Conscience is my best governor. God rules conscience. *Govern* and *gravy* were the words of our spelling-lesson which we talked about. . . . We talked with father about obedience. I liked the conversation and I think it will do me good."

The choice of a name for the little sister is an item chronicled with much interest, and on November 8, 1840, Anna writes, "We are going to name the baby Abby, after Mother." And it was then decided that the youngest child should be called Abba May Alcott, after one who was also the youngest of her family.

Little May's first Thanksgiving was celebrated by the family with strict simplicity, which must at times have awakened childish longings, for Anna wrote of it, upon November 26, "It was Thanksgiving today but we did not eat as other people do, but we had an apple-pudding for dinner."

That the enjoyment of their simple repasts was at times regulated in accordance with their attention to their lessons, is evinced by another entry, which reads, "I and Louisa did not spell our lesson well, so father let us go without any dinner."

The privilege of taking care of tiny May was viewed as a much-prized reward, and Anna writes a few weeks later:

"Father read and talked to us about curing our bad habits. I made a resolution and hope I shall keep it; he said that till we could be gentle and kind to each other we could not have the pleasure of tending baby. I had rather have most any other punishment than that. She is a sweet little thing and I love her very much."

A characteristic letter from Mrs. Alcott, written to her eldest daughter on Christmas Eve, touches upon this supervision of the little sister:

Your Christmas day will be a happy one just as far as you make it a good one. The presence of your little baby sister will make it merry if you give her your soft bosom for her pillow, and your sweet voice for her music. She was not with us last Christmas, let us be happier for her sake than we ever were before. Let us be patient because she is tender; let us be gentle because she is an angel and may put out her little wings and flutter back to God who only gave her to us to

make us happy on Earth. Love your sister Louisa
and be patient, love Elizabeth and be gentle, love
Abby and be kind, love Father and be obedient,
love Mother and be dutiful. Love your duty and
you will be happy.

MOTHER

Christmas Eve — 1840.

Mrs. Alcott's suggestion, "let us be happier for
her sake than ever before", strikes the keynote
of May's relationship to the others. Her special
contribution was to be one of joy, brightness, and
cheer. They were happier and gayer because of
May, her talents, her lively enthusiasm, and her
love of beauty. Her vivid personality radiated
sunshine, energy, and abundant life, which more
than compensated for those faults which belonged
to an impetuous nature prone to express itself in
occasional bursts of anger or impatience, and ani-
mated by an intense determination to carry out
its own pet projects.

May was indeed the "Queen", and in Louisa's
early descriptions of childish pranks the baby sister
seemed naturally to mount the throne, while the
others assumed humble positions. One recalls with
amusement the picture of that memorable occasion when Margaret Fuller and Emerson had spent
the afternoon discussing education with the elder

Alcotts, at the close of which conversation Miss Fuller exclaimed: "Well, Mr. Alcott, you have been able to carry out your methods in your own family, and I should like to see your model children." And Louisa writes:

"She did in a few minutes, for as the guests stood on the doorsteps a wild uproar approached, and round the corner of the house came a wheelbarrow holding baby May arrayed as a queen; I was the horse, bitted and bridled, and driven by my elder sister Anna; while Lizzie played dog, and barked as loud as her gentle voice permitted.

"All were shouting and wild with fun, which, however, came to a sudden end as we espied the stately group before us; for my foot tripped, and down we all went in a laughing heap; while my mother put a climax to the joke by saying, with a dramatic wave of the hand, 'Here are the model children, Miss Fuller'."

Baby May's first journey to the community at Fruitlands was in later years pictured by her sister Louisa in "Transcendental Wild Oats," where the writer describes the removal of the family, in June, 1843:

"A large wagon, drawn by a small horse and containing a motley load, went lumbering over certain New England hills with the pleasing accompaniment of wind, rain and hail. A serene man, with a serene child upon his knee, was driving, or rather being driven, for the small horse had it all his own way. A brown boy, with a William Penn countenance, sat beside him, firmly clasping a bust of Socrates. Behind them was an energetic looking woman, with a benevolent brow, satirical mouth, and eyes full of hope and courage. A baby reposed upon her lap, a mirror leaned against her knee, and a basket of provisions danced about her feet, as she struggled with a large unruly umbrella. Two blue-eyed little girls, with hands full of childish treasures, sat under one old shawl, chatting happily together.

"There was no road leading to the house, which could be seen that rainy afternoon through the blur of the landscape, and there is no doubt that the large wagon and the small horse floundered helplessly in the mud many times on the journey, until they drew up at last before the old red farmhouse, which was to be their home, just as a beautiful rainbow broke through the gray sky at the close of the day. So, looking on this as an omen of good cheer, the little girls sprang from the wagon in high spirits, and the older people followed, with baskets, bundles, umbrella and baby."

THE LITTLE MAY QUEEN

Thus did baby May make her entry into that visionary Utopia, which was relinquished after two years of pitiful effort to live there the life of the spirit with very little physical sustenance. One by one, Alcott's associates slipped away, and he, worn out in body and broken in spirit at the failure of the project, completely collapsed, and would hardly have survived the disappointment had not his brave wife and his little daughters rallied about him and helped to banish his despair. And then once more, baby May set forth on a journey back to the world that they had temporarily forsaken for the higher plane of "Fruitlands." This time there was no June rainbow with its promise of golden realization, but only fields of snow, when, on a bleak December day, the Alcott family emerged from the deep drifts that shut in the red farmhouse, bound for the nearest village of Still River, where Mrs. Alcott had engaged rooms for them in a house shared by their friends, the Love-joys. They proceeded on their way with all their worldly goods piled on an ox-sled, on the top of which were perched the four little daughters while the parents trudged behind. "Fruitlands", which Mrs. Alcott with her never-failing sense of humor had christened "Apple Slump", was a thing of the past.

Of its untimely passing, the author of "Little Women" said:

"The world was not ready for Utopia yet, and those who attempted to found it only got laughed at for their pains. In other days men could sell all and give all to the poor, lead lives devoted to holiness and high thought, and after the persecution was over find themselves honored as saints and martyrs. But in modern times, these things are out of fashion. To live for one's principles, at all costs, is a dangerous speculation; and the failure of an ideal no matter how humane and noble, is harder for the world to forgive and forget than bank robbery, or the grand swindles of corrupt politicians."

If at this time the family fortunes were at the lowest ebb, the baby girl was too young to be conscious of the cares and responsibilities that weighed upon her mother and sisters. Meanwhile, the eldest daughter, Anna (known to the world of little readers as "Meg"), from early childhood shared her mother's burdens, and from the first almost adopted May as her own baby, giving her the care and attention which Mrs. Alcott's many household duties made it impossible for her to render.

These responsibilities so willingly assumed by Anna were early shared by Louisa, who was two years her junior. In her quaint little journals, the younger sister writes of that busy life at "Fruitlands", when she was ten years old:

"I rose at five, and after breakfast washed the dishes, and then helped mother with the work. Miss F. is gone, and Anna in Boston with cousin Louisa. I took care of Abby in the afternoon. In the evening I made some pretty things for my dolly."

The menu which accompanied their idealistic régime she later described:

"Unleavened bread, porridge, and water for breakfast; bread, vegetables and water for dinner; bread, fruit, and water for supper was the bill-of-fare ordained by the elders. No teapot profaned that sacred stove, no gory steak cried aloud for vengeance from her chaste gridiron; and only a brave woman's taste, time and temper were sacrificed on that domestic altar."

The hours for play were very limited in those days when the struggle for existence was so acute as to place on the shoulders of the two eldest daughters many duties which even their little sister Beth strove to share with them. Yet, despite household tasks and strict economies, coupled with numerous small privations, the children learned to escape from daily drudgeries into a world of romance and imagination, and after the failure of the community at "Fruitlands" and their return to Concord, they roamed the fields and woods, enjoying all the natural beauties, taking part in games with their small neighbors, and acting little plays in the old barn at "Hillside", where they reveled in fancied luxury and splendor.

"Hillside", later the home of Hawthorne, who rechristened it "The Wayside", was purchased in 1845, with a small amount of money which had been left to Mrs. Alcott by her father, to which their ever-generous friend, Ralph Waldo Emerson, had added five hundred dollars. This house was only a short distance from Emerson's, and there Louisa and her sisters enjoyed the happy days described in "Little Women."

Beth's journal, which begins soon after their removal to this home, also describes her play-days with her little sister, May, then five years old.

Sunday, April 19, 1846.

Father walked in the woods with us. We saw some pretty trees to set out in the yard. I read in the "White Rose", and cleared my trunk. We went on the hill to see the rainbow, it was very beautiful. Abba and I went to the brook. I sewed a little in Louisa's room. . . . I read to Abba about Oliver Twist. She cried because he was so poor.

The following day she writes:

"I picked blue violets and dandelions. At ten I came in to school and wrote my journal for Sunday, and this morning I did some sums in Division, and read a piece of poetry. It was the 'Blind Boy.' In the afternoon, Abba and I sewed. She invited Mary Gill to come in to see her. I knit a little, and played with my dollies. Ellen and Edith [Emerson] came to see us. I went home with them. When I got back, I walked by Mr. Bull's with Abba to Mrs. Richardson's and drew her baby in the little wagon. The air was very cool."

"We were going to trim the May-Pole for to-morrow which is the first of May, but it rained. I was very sorry. I played with Abba a while, then came into school. My sums did not come right. I wrote the Multiplication Table on my slate from memory, and found I knew it all, and could think of it quick. Abba and I played house.

"Miss Foord came with Ellen to trim the May

Pole, for it had cleared off. Ellen and I picked violets on the hill."

The Maypole exercises are further described:

"After breakfast Miss Foord, and Cary Pratt, and Ellen, came to march with the May Pole, but Father took us in Mr. Watt's hay-cart to Mr. Emerson's. We danced round the May Pole, and I had a very pleasant time. Mr. Emerson said he would take us to ride in the woods. It rained, so we came back home. After the shower, Abba and I played in the barn. We made dirt-cakes, and a little wagon to draw our dollies in."

Beth's journal goes on to picture those happy summer days when she and Abba, who at this time seemed to be her special charge, played games together, and visited their friends, spending much time with the small Emersons, and at one period going to their home to study with their teacher, Miss Foord, regarding whom she writes:

"Miss Foord told us about the parts of strawberries. I told her one of my thoughts, which was 'I thought it was very shady at Sleepy Hollow.' Abba and I did not go to school this morning. We dressed our dollies and made the beds. We buried a little bird. Abba and I played school and made a little garden. We planted some corn and beans in it. . . . We all went again to Mr. Emersons. Father read to us about 'Maho and Zalmi.' I liked it very much. He talked with us about Contentment, and asked us when we were contented, and we all told. Mother, Louisa and Llewellyn were there and told. I said, I was, last winter in school. . . . I read Abba a story of a Fairy and a Golden Tree. We painted a good while."

One may fancy little Abba at this time, paint-brush in hand, foreshadowing her subsequent vocation, and frequent references to the children's enjoyment of drawing, figure in the journal, where Beth notes:

"My next lesson was drawing. I drew a flower, and two Angel kisses with long hair and wings, and robes. After dinner I played with Abba, and sewed till four."

The ending of the lessons at the Emerson's is mentioned:

"Abba and I are not going to Miss Foord's school any more, so Anna kept school for us at home. . . . At recess Louisa wheeled us in the wheelbarrow down the hill. . . . After dinner I washed the dishes and read a little in 'Arabian Nights', about a Prince. . . . I read Abba a story in the evening. Abba and I played in Mother's chamber. I was a sick lady and Abba was a doctor."

The journal for the year ends with the words, "I now have finished my journal and am going to give it to Mother."

Mrs. Alcott shared her husband's belief in the efficacy of keeping a diary of daily doings, and she faithfully followed her husband's example in this respect. She pens her commendation of Beth's work in the following words:

"It helps you to express them [your thoughts] and to understand your little self. Remember, dear girl, that a diary should be an epitome of your life. May it be a record of pure thoughts and actions, then you will indeed be the precious child of your loving mother."

If the education of the Alcott children was desultory and lacking in thoroughness in certain branches, it was in other ways inspiring and stimulating, developing their powers of imagination, and love of beauty in art and literature as well as nature, while teaching them to feel and to think justly, and to express their thoughts and feelings clearly and forcibly, even if they knew little of the rules of grammar and rhetoric.

CHAPTER II

The Young Artist

ALTHOUGH the ownership of "Hillside" provided the Alcott family with a pleasant abiding-place and a roof over their heads, yet there were six mouths to be fed, and Mr. Alcott's social ideals and exalted philosophy failed to secure the necessary wherewithal to feed and clothe the members of his household. Both Anna and Louisa strove hard to reinforce the family exchequer, but Concord offered little opportunity for work such as they seemed best fitted to perform, and so in 1848 the family removed to Boston, where for almost a decade the struggle for existence continued.

During this time, Bronson Alcott began to hold "Conversations" in West Street, where he assembled a small circle of intellectual persons who enjoyed his inspiring talks, discussed his theories, and a few of whom paid him a modest fee. Meanwhile Mrs. Alcott established an intelligence bureau, which had grown out of her interest in helping the needy to find positions, and at the same time Anna and Louisa were able to earn something by teaching and sewing, the latter, in 1852, receiving five dollars for her first published story, written some years before. At this time, Lizzie was called the "little housekeeper" and aided her mother in the domestic tasks, while the youngest daughter was sent to school.

May's earliest letters, written about this time, are very characteristic, and at the age of eight reflect her keen sense of the beautiful, her warmly affectionate nature, and her desire for pretty things. Throughout them, one discerns a little touch of the spoiled child, flashes of childish impatience, and keen displeasure at any failure to receive what she regarded as her rightful due.

The following letter, written prior to their removal to Boston, was sent to Mrs. Alcott during a visit made by her at Waterford, Connecticut. The writing seems to be in Mr. Alcott's hand, to whom the letter was evidently dictated:

July 5, 1848.

My dear Mother,—O mother, it is so beautiful this morning as I sit in the schoolroom by Father; such bright sunshine all about. Is it pleasant at Waterford as it is here? I will tell you about my lessons this morning. I came in right after breakfast, and read three stories in the book Mr. Farrer gave me: one of them was a long story about

John's being run away with in the chaise and
having his leg and arm broke.

I spelt 30 words all right and wrote down 22 on
my slate and numbered them in figures. Father
read me some pretty stories about Roses, how the
little boy was impatient to have the buds open,
and see the colors, and so picked the bud open,
and the leaves withered. I like to have Father
read stories to me and talk to me. I mean to have
my lessons quick after breakfast while the girls
are doing up the work. Father has your miniature
on his desk where he can see it as he opens his
desk every morning. And you look stately. I
have just been looking at it. I wish you would
come home soon; when will you come? I guess
Father wants to see you now too. We went to the
fire-works last evening. They were before Col.
Shattuck's house on the Common, and all the
Concord people (to say "folks" seems countryfied)
were there; some came in chaises and sat in them
to see the fire-works go up. Father took us all to
see them, and we stood before the Court House by
the wall to look. I liked the whirligigs. The boys
cracked off powder-crackers all about us. One
almost hit my heel. We have beautiful tableaux
now in the barn. One was William Tell. I was
the little boy, and Louisa the Father. We had

the cross man and wife, and the "Margiana." How does Mason do? He is very handsome. You told me about my little hood and coat. You do not write to me. Is it because you have so much to do? Do you care nothing about me? I do for you.

This is a long letter; longer a great deal than I wanted to write, but Father kept asking me more and more questions, till it seemed as if he would never be done, and so filled this letter — I am glad he has got through.

Good bye, Good Mother.

From ABBY

At the end of this letter Mr. Alcott writes, after the words, "From Abby", "with her feet on the table by the window, laughing through her tears; and father laughing at the fun too."

This youthful production was followed by an aggrieved note, dictated the following afternoon, when the mail had brought no letter for "Abba May."

DEAR MOTHER,—O, I was so disappointed when Father told me there was no letter for me that I cried right out. I could not help it. I felt jealous. The girls all had letters, but there was no letter for me. You said I should have one next week and

I am waiting for it. I wish you would come home. But Anna has come and we have such good times to have her teach us. We had a nice ride by the cottage chamber where I was born. I remember Fruitlands, and Mr. Lovejoy; we were scalded. The house at Fruitlands was long and red. My memory is short. I had a pretty ride and pleasant. The strawberries and cream were very nice. I picked one row of strawberries. I wanted the gilt greyhound lying on the white marble that Anna brought home and gave to Elizabeth, it was so handsome.

I should like to see Charlotte Dingley and send her my love. I wish I had staid with you. Father asked me if I worried you, and that made me cry; it seemed unkind. It seems as if I did not very often. I don't want to tell him any more to write. I shall not send the least bit of love till you write to me.

From Abby to Mother.

Those that are prone to think of Mrs. Alcott merely as a warm-hearted practical woman, absorbed in household tasks, fail to realize her superior intellectual qualities. She wielded a gifted pen, kept pace with her husband's philosophy and ideals, and could dwell on his plane of thought

even while keeping her own feet firmly planted on
the level ground of everyday living.

Her gifted husband meanwhile was, as his
daughter Louisa remarked, up in a balloon, with
all the family holding the strings and trying to
pull him down to earth.

"Little Raphael's" gift for drawing, which developed early, gave her family much satisfaction
as well as some anxiety at times, as her experi-
ments in certain instances threatened the safety
of the household, experiences later recorded by
her sister in the descriptions of "Amy's artistic
efforts":

"She was never so happy as when copying
flowers, designing fairies, or illustrating stories with
queer specimens of art. Her teacher complained
that instead of doing her sums she covered her
slate with animals; the blank pages of her atlas
were used to copy maps on, and caricatures of the
most ludicrous description came fluttering out of
her books at unlucky moments. She got through
her lessons as well as she could, and managed
to escape reprimands by being a model of deport-
ment. She was a great favorite with her mates,
being good-tempered, and possessing the happy
art of pleasing without effort. Her little airs and

graces were much admired, so were her accomplishments; for beside her drawing she could play twelve tunes, crochet and read French without mispronouncing more than two-thirds of the words. She had a plaintive way of saying 'When papa was rich, we did so and so', which was very touching; and her long words were considered 'perfectly elegant', by the girls."

Her little vanities were also humorously touched upon:

"If anybody had asked Amy what the greatest trial of her life was, she would have answered at once, 'my nose' . . . It was not big, nor red, like poor Petrea's; it was only rather flat, and all the pinching in the world could not give it an aristocratic point. No one minded it but herself, and it was doing its best to grow, but Amy felt deeply the want of a Grecian nose, and drew whole sheets of handsome ones to console herself."

No better picture of May's early efforts in the field of art can be supplied than that penned by her sister, who continues:

"It takes people a long time to learn the difference between talent and genius, especially ambitious young men and women. Amy was learning this distinction through much tribulation; for, mistaking enthusiasm for inspiration, she attempted every branch of art with youthful audacity. For a long time there was a lull in the 'mud-pie' business, and she devoted herself to the finest pen-and-ink drawing, in which she showed such taste and skill, that her graceful handiwork proved both pleasant and profitable. But over-strained eyes soon caused pen-and-ink to be laid aside for a bold attempt at poker-sketching. While this attack lasted, the family lived in constant fear of a conflagration; for the odor of burning wood pervaded the house at all hours; smoke issued from attic and shed with alarming frequency, red-hot pokers lay about promiscuously, and Hannah never went to bed without a pail of water and the dinner-bell at her door, in case of fire. Raphael's face was found boldly executed on the under side of a mouldering board [this clever burnt-wood picture may now be seen at Orchard House], and Bacchus on the head of a beer-barrel; a chanting cherub adorned the cover of the sugar-bucket, and attempts to portray 'Garrick buying gloves of the grisette', supplied kindlings for some time.

"From fire to oil was a natural transition for burnt fingers, and Amy fell to painting with undiminished ardor. An artist friend fitted her out with his cast-off palettes, brushes, and colors, and she daubed away, producing pastoral and marine views, such as were never seen on land or sea.

"Her monstrosities in the way of cattle would have taken prizes at an agricultural fair; and the perilous pitching of her vessels would have produced sea-sickness in the most nautical observer, if the utter disregard of all known rules of ship-building and rigging had not convulsed him with laughter at the first glance. Swarthy boys and dark-eyed Madonnas staring at you from one corner of the studio, did not suggest Murillo; oily brown shadows of faces, with a lurid streak in the wrong place, meant Rembrandt; buxom ladies and dropsical infants, Rubens; and Turner appeared in tempests of blue thunder, orange lightning, brown rain, and purple clouds, with a tomato-colored splash in the middle which might be the sun, or a buoy, a sailor's shirt or a king's robe, as the spectator pleased."

May's early admiration for Turner's paintings, here touched upon, was destined to find expression in some of her best work, for her most admirable copies of this master's pictures, made during faithful study at the National Gallery in London, won highest commendation from Ruskin, and caused her copies to be later used as guides for students. Her early attempts at portraiture are also entertainingly set forth by her sister:

"Charcoal portraits came next; and the entire family hung in a row, looking as wild and crocky as if just evoked from a coal-bin. Softened into crayon sketches, they did better; for the likenesses were good, and Amy's hair, Jo's nose, Meg's mouth, and Laurie's eyes were pronounced 'wonderfully fine.' A return to clay and plaster followed, and ghostly casts of her acquaintances haunted corners of the house, or tumbled off closet shelves on to people's heads. Children were enticed in as models, till their incoherent accounts of her mysterious doings caused Miss Amy to be regarded in the light of a young ogress. Her efforts in this line, however, were brought to an abrupt close by an untoward accident, which quenched her ardor. Other models failing her for a time, she undertook to cast her own pretty foot, and the family were one day alarmed by an unearthly bumping and screaming; and, running to the rescue, found the young enthusiast hopping wildly about the shed, with her foot held fast in a pan full of plaster, which had hardened with unexpected rapidity.

With much difficulty and some danger, she was dug out; for Jo was so overcome with laughter while she excavated, that her knife went too far, cut the poor foot, and left a lasting memorial of one artistic attempt at least."

This semi-tragic episode was often recalled with mirth by members of the Alcott family, and the cast of May's foot may still be seen at Orchard House, among the varying examples of the young artist's early work. Louisa's recital of her sister's further efforts continues:

"After this Amy subsided, till a mania for sketching from nature set her to haunting river, field and wood, for picturesque studies, and sighing for ruins to copy. She caught endless colds sitting on damp grass to book 'a delicious bit', composed of a stone, a stump, one mushroom and a broken mullein stalk, or a 'heavenly mass of clouds', that looked like a choice display of feather-beds when done. She sacrificed her complexion floating on the river in the midsummer sun, to study light and shade, and got a wrinkle over her nose, trying after 'points of sight', or whatever the squint and string performance is called.

"If 'genius is eternal patience', as Michael Angelo affirms, Amy certainly had some claims to the divine attribute, for she persevered in spite of all obstacles, failures and discouragements, firmly believing that in time she should do something worthy to be called 'high art'."

The above quotation, referred to in his introductory sketch, by Mr. French, is in truth highly applicable to May, whether it emanated from the brain of an Alcott or an Angelo. Louisa ends her summary of her sister's "artistic attempts" with a brief reference to her personal attributes:

"She was learning, doing and enjoying other things, meanwhile, for she had resolved to be an attractive and accomplished woman, even if she never became a great artist. Here she succeeded better; for she was one of those happily created beings who please without effort, make friends everywhere, and take life so gracefully and easily that less fortunate souls are tempted to believe that such are born under a lucky star. Everybody liked her, for among her good gifts was tact. She had an instinctive sense of what was pleasing and proper, always said the right thing to the right person, did just what suited the time and place, and was so self-possessed that her sisters used to say, 'If Amy went to court without any rehearsal beforehand, she'd know exactly what to do'."

MAY ALCOTT

May's social gifts, here truthfully portrayed, doubtless had much to do with her success in later years, in winning friends upon all sides, wherever she might be. And though she never figured at the court of St. James, her charm and quick responsiveness brought her a widespread popularity at home, and also among her fellow artists abroad.

Few characters in fiction have secured such a following as that accorded to the impetuous, affectionate, and gifted "Amy" of "Little Women", who, from her first appearance in the world of letters, was recognized as being so veritably alive that hosts of youthful readers came to regard her as a household friend, followed her doings with the keenest interest, and showered Louisa Alcott with inquiries as to her origin and subsequent career. Thousands of times the authoress was forced to respond to such demands, with the assurance that "Amy" was absolutely true to life, and that she did *not* marry "Laurie."

If, as depicted in the book, the other sisters were in truth little "women", May was undoubtedly a little "lady", a fact that all the others recognized and respected. From earliest childhood, as has been stated, she was continually striving towards her ideal of elegance and beauty, the absence of which qualities in her home life caused her considerable distress and mortification. Meanwhile, the others, conscious of her fastidiousness, strove to supply these painful deficiencies. And from the first there was a species of unwritten law which decreed that although her sisters wore shabby frocks, May must, if possible, have something new. And the returns from Louisa's earliest stories, scant though they were, seldom failed to supply some purchase for the little sister. The following extract from a letter written by the young authoress to Anna, in 1855, presents this point of view:

"I have eleven dollars, all my own earnings, five for a story, and four for the pile of sewing I did for Dr. Gray's society, to give him as a present. . . . I got a crimson ribbon for a bonnet for May, and I took my straw and fixed it nicely with some little duds I had. Her old one has haunted me all winter, and I want her to look neat. She is so graceful and pretty and loves beauty so much, it is hard for her to be poor and wear other peoples' things. You and I have learned not to mind *much*; but when I think of her, I long to dash out and buy her the finest hat the limited sum of ten dollars can procure. She says so sweetly in one of her letters, 'It is hard sometimes to see other people have so many nice things and I so few, but I try not to be envious, but contented with my poor clothes and cheerful about it'."

Louisa concludes:

"I hope the dear will like the bonnet and the frill, and some bows I made from some bright ribbons L. W. threw away. I get half my rarities from her rag-bag, and she does n't know her own rags when fixed over. I hope I shall live to see the dear child in silk and lace with plenty of pictures and 'bottles of cream', Europe and all she longs for."

And by Louisa's gifted pen this hope was subsequently realized, as was her ambition to give her mother the ease and comforts she longed to bestow, and concerning which she wrote:

"I think often what a hard life she has had since she married, so full of wandering and all sorts of worry. So different from her early days, the youngest and most petted of the family. I think she is a very brave, good woman; and my dream is to have a lovely quiet home for her, with no debts or troubles to burden her. But I'm afraid she will be in Heaven before I can do it."

THE YOUNG ARTIST

During this strenuous epoch in Boston, when their modest home was converted into a shelter for lost girls, abused wives, and friendless children, not to mention weak and wicked men, Mr. and Mrs. Alcott, who had no gold to give, gave their time, sympathy, and help, and in return for their unselfish deeds acquired a number of contagious diseases for their own children.

Although too young to share in lifting the financial burdens that early rested on her elder sisters' shoulders, little May, who had a keenly practical mind, was conscious of the fact that her father's philosophy failed to bring in material returns, and the thought that he lectured and then brought home no money, aroused her youthful indignation. That she, more than the others, was ready to urge him to be more businesslike was evident from the first. She was only twelve when he returned from a trip to the West, which has been frequently described. A hungry, weary, and half-frozen wanderer, he appeared late one wintry night after his family had retired, and as they sprang from their beds to minister to his bodily needs, none dared to voice the thought that hovered in all their minds, namely, "Had he made any money on this trip?" Then it was that the voice of little May was heard inquiring, "Well, did the people pay you?" In response to which, he opened his pocketbook and showed them one lonely dollar bill, saying, "My overcoat was stolen and I had to buy a shawl. Many promises were not kept, and traveling is costly, but I have opened the way, and another year shall do better."

Then, as has often been recorded, the loving wife, who had only words of sympathy to offer, exclaimed, "I call that doing very well. Since you are safely home, dear, we don't ask anything more."

But there was bitter disappointment in the hearts of the children, who were expecting much from their father's trip; and one may rest assured that "Little Raphael's" pillow was that night wet with tears.

While this daughter's youth freed her from sharing the financial responsibilities during these years of stress, it did not bring her immunity from the various diseases acquired by the Alcott children as a result of philanthropic zeal on the part of their parents. There was a siege with smallpox, contracted in the efforts to shelter the afflicted, and in 1856, May and Elizabeth ("Beth") were stricken with scarlet fever, from the effects of which the latter never fully recovered, dying two years later after months of failing health. This contagion was brought into the household by some poor children

who were nursed by Mrs. Alcott, when they fell
ill from living in a wretched unsanitary hovel.
Their landlord (alas, a deacon!) had refused to
improve conditions, but was finally forced to do so
by Mrs. Alcott, who paid too dearly for her act of
kindness.

The autumn of this year, 1856, found Louisa in
Boston, settled in a tiny bedroom at Mrs. David
Reed's boarding house in Chauncy Street, described in "Little Women" as "Jo's Garret." A
happy winter for her followed, as well as one of
strenuous work; and at this time she enjoyed the
friendship of Theodore Parker, who advised and
encouraged her in the pursuance of her literary
work, for which there was an increasing demand.
It was a satisfaction to Louisa to have her sister
May also in Boston for the winter, and it was
arranged that she should meanwhile study art,
making her home with an aunt who lived in the
city.

And on November 14, 1856, Louisa wrote:

"May came full of expectation and joy to visit
good Aunt Bond, and study drawing. We walked
about and had a good home talk, then my girl
went off to Auntie's to begin what I hope will
be a pleasant and profitable winter. She needs

help to develop her talent, and I can't give it to her."

A few days later, she speaks of attending a little party at her Aunt's house, where May looked very pretty and seemed to be a special favorite.

And now Louisa was beginning to prove the truth of assertion, that "though an Alcott, she could support herself." Her literary gift was steadily gaining recognition, although it was to be almost a decade before she could achieve the hoped-for success, and realize her ambition to make her dear ones comfortable and free from monetary anxiety. Especially did she desire to give the gifted May the longed-for opportunities.

At this time May was studying music, French, and drawing, thus preparing herself to be, as this sister desired, "an accomplished Alcott." Her skill with pen and pencil became more and more evident, and when she returned to Concord in the spring, she had completed a season of successful work, and brought back with her, among many other sketches, an admirable crayon head of her mother, a gift which filled the heart of "Marmee" with pride and joy.

CHAPTER III

The Sisters

THE opening months of the year 1857 saw the young writer of twenty-five ensconced in her attic room at Mrs. Reed's boarding house in Boston, and slowly gaining a foothold in the field of letters; there she was temporarily free from household cares, which were assumed by Anna, the domestic angel; while May, at sixteen, was rapidly proving that faith in her artistic gift was not misplaced. Meanwhile, the increasing illness of the gentle and unworldly Elizabeth cast a gloom over all.

The passing of Beth, as told in "Little Women", presents with truthfulness the story of her gradual decline, and the great sorrow of the family in watching this delicate girl fade from their sight; although she lingered until March, 1858, they had learned months before that they must let her go.

In September, 1857, Orchard House was purchased, but it was not ready for occupancy until the following spring. This purchase marked an epoch in the history of the Alcott family, for in this house they spent their happiest years; there Mr. Alcott founded his famous School of Philosophy, and there Louisa produced her masterpieces.

There, also, May established her studio, and traces of her household decoration throughout the house still attest to her early accomplishments in the artistic field. The well-preserved old structure, occupied by the Alcotts for twenty years, is now a permanent literary shrine, filled with the Alcott memorabilia, and likely to be visited for years to come by countless pilgrims.

But Beth was not destined to dwell beneath the friendly roof of Orchard House, which was at the time of its purchase so sadly out of repair that months must needs pass ere it could be ready for occupancy. In consequence, the family rented a portion of another house, and there Beth spent the last of her brief life, lying upon her couch before the fire, reading, and singing softly to herself, patient and sweet, while Anna did the housekeeping, and Mrs. Alcott and Louisa devoted themselves to ministering to the wants of their invalid.

Beth slipped away on March 14, 1858, after bidding them all good-by, and murmuring with a happy smile, "All here." So peaceful was her passing that after she had gone Louisa wrote, "Death never seemed terrible to me, and now is beautiful; so I cannot fear it, but find it friendly and wonderful."

THE SISTERS

At the moment of Beth's passing, a curious psychic phenomenon was noted by the watchers, Louisa and her mother, which was immediately recorded in the former's journal of March 14, 1858.

Louisa wrote that after bidding all good-by, the sick girl lapsed into unconsciousness, and then she added:

"A few moments after the last breath came, as Mother and I sat silently watching the shadow fall on the dear little face, I saw a light mist rise from her body, and float up and vanish in the air. Mother's eyes followed mine and when I said, 'What did you see?' she described the same light mist. Dr. G. said it was life departing visibly."

The death of the lovely, unworldly Beth cast a gloom over all the household, and saddened the days preceding the settling in the new home; a process destined to furnish plentiful occupation and diversion.

Following Beth's passing, came the announcement of the engagement of Anna to John Pratt, which meant the slipping from the family circle of another sister. From this time May and Louisa drew still more closely together, and the latter found much comfort in the companionship of the lively young artist, whose swift responsiveness and cheery personality did much towards banishing the heavy clouds that rested on the household. May was warmly affectionate and adored her sister's brilliant qualities, believing at the same time in her own gifts, and being quite convinced that some day she would show the world a second famous Alcott sister.

In July, 1858, the family took possession of the new house, which was in truth a very old one — so old that when the place was purchased by the Alcotts, the house (built about 1650) was thought to be so antiquated and out of repair that it was practically thrown in as a bargain, in the belief that it was only fit for firewood.

But Mr. Alcott, who had a decided architectural gift, realized its possibilities, and finding the old beams and rafters firm, felt no hesitation in attempting the renovation of the structure. He set about converting old ovens and ash holes into arched alcoves and attractive nooks, and the result was a surprise and satisfaction to all concerned. And to the father's architectural efforts the daughters added countless practical touches and bits of decoration. They painted, papered, and carpentered, preparing the interior with their own hands, while Mr. Alcott expended his ingenuity on the exterior. In nooks and corners, May placed effective panels on which she painted birds and flowers; over the fireplaces, she inscribed mottoes in Old English characters, choosing for the chimney piece in her father's study, the lines of Ellery Channing:

The Hills are reared, the Valleys scooped in vain,
If Learning's Altars vanish from the Plain.

May fairly reveled in the process of working decorative wonders, and those that to-day visit Orchard House delight to study the many remaining traces of her brush, pen, and pencil, as well as the examples of her work in clay. Walls, doors, and window-casings in several rooms still bear her outline drawings, while other memorabilia remain upon the walls.

During the summer of 1858, May worked industriously, and illustrated her first book, a little story by Louisa, entitled "Christmas Elves." The autumn saw the latter again in Boston, engaged in literary work, and there May joined her, continuing her drawing lessons, and attending the School of Design. There her productions were highly praised, and she returned to Concord filled with enthusiasm for her work, which was an ever-increasing satisfaction to the family. While they depended upon Louisa as their mainstay, they were particularly proud of the young artist, whose modeling, as well as drawing, seemed to betoken a successful future in the world of art. About this time, May executed for Louisa a fine bas-relief copy of Mr. Emerson's favorite, "Endymion", of which her sister was very fond. In the spring of 1860, Anna's marriage to John Pratt took place, upon May 23d, her mother's wedding day. This was a great event for all the family, and in describing it Louisa wrote:

"A lovely day; the house full of sunshine, flowers, friends and happiness. Uncle S. J. May married them with no fuss, but much love; and we all stood round her. She in her silver gray silk, with lilies-of-the-valley (John's flower) in her bosom and hair. We, in gray thin stuff, sackcloth I called it and ashes of roses; for I mourn my Nan, and am not comforted. We have had a little feast, sent by good Judge Shaw; then the old folks danced around the bridal pair on the lawn in the German fashion, making a pretty picture to remember, under our Revolutionary Elm.

"Then with tears and kisses, our dear girl, in her little white bonnet, went happily away with her good John; and we ended our first wedding."

So Louisa parted from her second sister, not dreaming that at the wedding of the remaining one the bride would be alone in a far land, without one of her own present to wish her happiness or to see her settled in her new home across the sea.

Louisa shared May's love of horseback riding, and they spent many invigorating hours together in the enjoyment of this pastime, of which the former wrote, in 1860:

"Made two riding-habits, and May and I had some fine rides. Both needed exercise, and this was really good for us. So one of our dreams came true, and we really did 'dash away on horseback'."

May's great enthusiasm for riding left in many minds the picture of the youngest Alcott daughter dashing about the country upon her favorite horse, often accompanied by local cavaliers, with whom she was most popular.

Louisa took an ever-increasing pride in the personal charms of her young sister, recording in her journal, "Made my first ball-dress for May, and she was the finest girl at the party, my tall, blonde, graceful girl! I was proud of her."

Her pleasure in this sister's "lucky star" (under which, all the family believed, she had been born) is noted by her in the following autumn, November, 1860:

"Kind Miss R. sent May $30 for lessons, so she went to Boston to take some of Johnston. She is one of the lucky ones and gets what she wants easily. I have to grind, or go without it. Good for me doubtless, or it would not be so. Cheer up, Louisa, and grind away!"

December brought more luck for May. She wanted to go to Syracuse to teach, and in answer to her wish, a friend of the family sent for her, at the suggestions of her uncle Samuel J. May, while Louisa sewed "like a steam-engine" for a week, getting her sister's things ready, and on December 17th accompanied her to Boston to see her off by rail on this her first venture away from home.

In August, she returned, very tired, but satisfied that her first experiment away from home had proved successful; Louisa noted her growing popularity, of which she wrote, "May is quite a belle now, and much improved, — a tall blonde lass, full of grace and spirit."

Among the Concord memories that cluster about this period, those pleasant evenings may be recalled when the Alcott girls joined with the Hawthorne household in playing games and in composing nonsense rhymes, a pastime much in vogue at that time. On one of these occasions Nathaniel Hawthorne took a piece of paper and scratched off the following lines, intended to amuse the daughters of Bronson Alcott:

There dwelt a Sage at Apple-Slump,
Whose dinner never made him plump;
Give him carrots, potatoes, squash, parsnips and peas,
Some boiled macaroni, without any cheese,
And a plate of raw apples to hold on his knees,
And a glass of sweet cider, to wash down all these,
And he'd prate of the Spirit as long as you'd please,
This airy Sage of Apple-Slump.

This production no doubt furnished the Sage's daughters with a burst of merriment, which helped to lighten those gloomy days when war clouds were gathering and many of Concord's brave sons were leaving for the front.

At this time, Mrs. Hawthorne wrote to her daughter Una, who was at Beverly:

"Great events seem thickening here. Louisa Alcott has had her summons to the Washington Hospitals; and Abbey came to ask me about some indelible ink she had, and I offered doing anything I could for Louisa. She said if I could mark her clothes it would assist her very much. So I went over, in the divine afternoon, and marked till dusk, and finished all she had."

What a touching picture these two notable mothers must have made, bending lovingly over those simple garments so soon to be transported to the scene of war, and marking each piece with the name, not of the *author*, but the *soldier*, "Louisa Alcott."

Sophia Hawthorne concludes her letter to Una with the words:

"Mrs. Alcott says she shall feel helpless without Louisa, and Mr. Alcott says he sends his only son. Louisa is determined to make the soldiers jolly, and takes all of Dickens that she has, and games. At supper-time Julian came in with the portentous news that the battle has at last begun, and Fredricksburg is on fire from our guns. So Louisa goes to the very mouth of the war. I carried to Mrs. Alcott early this morning some maizena blancmange, which Ann made for papa, and turned out of the sheaf-mould very nicely."

Thus with many little kindnesses did the Concord neighbors minister to one another in those anxious days when each New England town was contributing its best and bravest to its country.

On December 12, 1862, Louisa Alcott, whose patriotic spirit and tireless energy had made it impossible for her to sit at home while she felt that

her country needed her, began her career as a war
nurse after a brave farewell to her dear ones in Concord. To the members of her household who depended upon her strength and spirit, and realized the
risk she was about to take, the parting was a harrowing one; but they did not attempt to alter her decision.

Just at the last, her courage almost failed her,
and she embraced her mother crying, "Shall I
stay?" To which Mrs. Alcott answered through
her tears, "No, go! and the Lord be with you."

Then she departed in the December twilight,
being escorted to the station by May and her young
friend, Julian Hawthorne, who waved a sorrowful
farewell as she courageously set out upon her
journey to Washington to take her place in the
Union Hospital at Georgetown, where for six weeks
she worked untiringly, under those hard and painful conditions later described by her in "Hospital
Sketches."

Then as a result of overwork and unsanitary
conditions she broke down, stricken with typhoid-
pneumonia, from which she slowly crawled back to
life, never again to be the same hardy, robust
Louisa. Before that time, she had never known
what it was to be ill, and after it she was never
again absolutely well. So she gave to her country
ungrudgingly, as to her family, her very best.

After those strenuous weeks of ministering to the sick and dying had culminated in her own breakdown, Louisa's journey homeward remained to her but a vague memory; her father brought her back, and she recalled the vision of her sister May's shocked face as she stood waiting for her on the platform, at the Concord station, just where she had taken leave of her, as if perchance she might have been there watching all the while.

Then followed three weeks of delirium, and a slow convalescence; long nights and idle days with the devoted mother in attendance, and May singing or reading to entertain her. In March, Louisa rallied and sat up, cleaned up her piece bags, dusted her books, and mourned the cutting off of her beautiful hair, which had been one and a half yards long.

In April, she was able once more to take some pleasant walks and drives, and a month later resumed her work and aided May in putting the house in order during the absence of her mother, who was visiting her married daughter. Meanwhile May painted and papered the parlors, while Louisa bought rugs and a new carpet, thus furnishing a pleasant surprise for Mrs. Alcott on her return.

And now the publishers were more and more

desirous of contributions from Louisa's pen, and her literary earnings became more plentiful so that she made the cheery entry in her journal for October:

"There is a sudden hoist for the meek and lowly scribbler, who was told to 'stick to her teaching', and never had a literary friend to lend a helping hand. Fifteen years of hard grubbing may be coming to something after all; and I may be able to pay all the debts, fix the house, send May to Italy, and keep the old folks cozy."

The dream of sending her sister to Italy was not yet to be realized, but she could now bestow upon her more advantages; and in October, May began to take lessons of Doctor Rimmer, who was unexcelled as a teacher of anatomical drawing.

The new year found Louisa busy with her writing, and thankful that her past year's work had helped to pay the family expenses and to aid May's art studies, but a month later she was forced to relinquish her pen for household duties, as Nan was taken ill and Mrs. Alcott was again called away from home to nurse her.

During this time Louisa wrote of May's good fortune:

"Mrs. S. takes a great fancy to May, sends her flowers, offers to pay for her to go to the new art school, and arranges everything delightfully for her. She is a fortunate girl, and always finds some one to help her as she wants to be helped. Wish I could do the same, but suppose as I never do that it is best for me to work and wait and do all for myself."

Louisa's acceptance of drudgery and sacrifice as her special portion was at times productive of selfishness in others, who, had she been less self-effacing would have undoubtedly done more to conserve her strength.

One can feel only exasperation at reading in her journal:

"I feel very moral today, having done a big wash alone, baked, swept the house, picked the hops, got dinner, and written a chapter in 'Moods.' — May gets exhausted with work, though she walks six miles without a murmur."

Such jottings do much to convince one that if May was a little spoiled, Louisa had a hand in bringing this about.

May loved the things of life, and their possession brought her a joy so genuine that it fairly radiated from her, and shed its brightness on all about her, and their relinquishment, or any failure to attain them, meant bitter disappointment; whereas Louisa cared for things only when she knew they would contribute to some one's happiness and comfort. Money she wanted to buy freedom from care and peace of mind, not money to buy jewels, clothes, or works of art, which would have given May such joy.

Louisa reveled in May's delight and loved to give her pretty things, though for herself they did not greatly matter; and May, in turn, desired with all her heart to win success with her artistic gift, which she felt was no mean endowment, and to repay her sister in generous measure. She had implicit confidence in her own powers and in her lucky stars, — which were to aid her to come into her own.

And her stars shone propitiously, the sunlight danced about her path, and she moved happily and confidently on towards the goal which she was not destined to reach. She wanted fame and success in the world of art, and felt that she could win them; Louisa wanted neither, and they were hers without the asking. Yet if, as Stevenson has said, "It is better to travel pleasantly, than to arrive", no doubt May's portion was more to be desired.

And when, upon occasion, Louisa also "traveled pleasantly", she had invariably May's cheery companionship. In August, 1864, the sisters spent a delightful fortnight with friends at Gloucester, where a family of six pretty daughters added to the joys of the lively household. Louisa found their genial host a reminder of the "brothers Cheeryble"; and she and May indulged in a continual round of summer festivities, boating, dancing, picnicking, and taking part in the old-time charades. On one mild night, they camped out on the rocks, singing, talking, or napping, and there saw the moon rise and set in splendor, remaining to view the glories of the sunrise, which was a memorable experience.

Louisa's growing fame, and her endeavors to increase her literary output, while also shouldering home burdens, told on her health, already impaired by severe illness, and she longed for a change of scene. Her great desire was to see Europe, and when the chance arose to travel as the companion for a young friend, a semi-invalid, she promptly grasped the opportunity, and they journeyed for some months on the continent. Ere long, however, the care proved too much for Louisa Alcott, and she was forced to relinquish her charge, for although devotedly kind and unselfish she had not the temperament suited to the needs of a nervous invalid. After nine months, she gave up the position and traveled on alone to Paris and London, where she was greeted by many of her father's friends, and where her weeks of freedom found her "happy as a bird."

It was at this period that, at Vevay, she became well acquainted with an attractive Polish youth, Ladislas Wisinewski, who was a fellow boarder at the pension where she was staying. He had suffered imprisonment and hardship in the Polish Revolution, and he made her his confidant, and became an ardent adorer, bringing her flowers and calling her his "little mother." Although he was then twenty-five, and she but eight years older, she declared herself "a lofty spinster who loved him like a half-dozen grandmothers." She called him "Laddie", and sometimes "Laurie", acknowledging in after years that he was the model for the hero of "Little Women", although the widely beloved "Laurie" was really a composite of the dark-eyed foreigner and the flaxen-haired Alfred Whitman, who had come to Concord in 1857 to attend Mr. Sanborn's school. The latter youth lived in the home of the Pratt family and came to know the Alcotts shortly before Beth's death. He acted in the Concord Dramatic Club with Louisa, with whom he kept up a correspondence long after his return to his home in Kansas. And she afterwards wrote him regarding the hero of her book, "Bless your heart, I put you into my story as one of the best and dearest lads I ever knew. Laurie is you and my Polish boy jointly."

This trip abroad ended with a few happy weeks in London, where the traveler from Concord enjoyed association with many persons of distinction, who later became May's friends when she took up her art studies in London.

While visiting at Aubrey House, the lovely English home of Mr. and Mrs. Peter Taylor, Louisa met Jean Ingelow, Frances Power Cobb, Matilde Blinde, John Stuart Mill, Gladstone, John Bright, Thomas Hughes, and many others.

She also visited Mr. and Mrs. Moncure D. Conway, who were close family friends, and who later took the warmest interest in May's life in London.

On July 7, 1866, Louisa sailed back to her own country, having realized in part her dream of European travel, though little freedom in its enjoyment. After a stormy voyage she reached home considerably improved in health and ready once more to assume the family responsibilities.

She wrote of her return:

"Father at the station, Nan and the babies at the gate, May flying wildly round the lawn, and Marmee crying at the door. Into her arms I went and was at home at last. Happy days, talking and enjoying one another. Many people came to see me and said I was much improved, of which I was glad, for there was, is, and always will be room for it. Found Mother looking old, sick and tired; Father as placid as ever. Nan poorly, but blest in her babies; May full of plans as usual."

Then followed a year of strenuous literary work for Louisa, while May pursued her art studies, and together they assumed the added household duties, which Mrs. Alcott's frail health made more confining.

The autumn of 1867 found Louisa hard at work, after a brief vacation trip, striving to supply the family with money and the publishers with copy. Then in September, Mr. Thomas Niles, a partner of the firm of Roberts Brothers, asked her to write a book for girls. It was a crucial question and she replied, "I'll try."

A few weeks later she was settled in Boston for the winter, where she could work uninterruptedly, and where she enjoyed better health than in Concord. The picture of her journey thither well supplements that earlier vision of the Alcott family riding to Fruitlands with their household gods.

In "An Old-Fashioned Girl" she has described the latter trip taken in company with her nephew Fred:

"You ought to have seen my triumphal entry into the city, sitting among my goods and chattels, in a farmer's cart, on my little sofa, with boxes and bundles all around me, a bird-cage on one side, a fishing-basket, with a kitten's head popping out of the hole on the other side."

She tells of many bumps and jolts experienced in the unconventional equipage, and of the bookshelf tumbling on to her head during a steep descent, while a pet rocking chair slid off behind them as they ascended another hill. And with these household furnishings, Louisa arranged her sunny room at Number 6 Hayward Place, where she was joined by May, who soon established several drawing classes which brought her a satisfactory return. They enjoyed their "light housekeeping", and often entertained their friends at twilight, around a cheerful blaze, dispensing tea and buttered toast. Dickens was at this time delivering his final Boston readings, and for him they both cherished an intense enthusiasm. Louisa, who always delighted in theatricals, was able to indulge her taste in that direction, and also to figure in her favorite rôle of Mrs. Jarley, who, with her famous waxworks, was a popular feature in many entertainments at that period.

In January, 1868, Louisa wrote:

"The year begins well and cheerfully for us all. Father and Mother comfortable at home; Anna and family settled in Chelsea; May busy with her drawing classes, of which she has five or six, and the prospect of earning $150 a quarter; also she is well and in good spirits. I am in my room, spending busy, happy days, because I have quiet, freedom, work enough, and strength to do it."

She concludes with the words:

"For many years we have not been so comfortable. May and I are both earning. Anna with her good John to lean on, and the old people with a cozy home of their own. Today, my first hyacinth blossomed, white and sweet, — a good omen, — a little flag of truce, perhaps, from the enemies whom we have been fighting all these years. Perhaps we are to win after all, and conquer poverty, neglect, pain and debt, and march on with flags flying into the New World with the New Year."

MAY ALCOTT

In view of the present much-deplored social conditions among those of the youthful generation, it may be edifying to record Louisa's anxiety concerning a member of her younger sister's social circle at this period:

"Talked half the night with H. A. about the fast ways of young people nowadays, and gave the child much older sisterly advice, as no one seems to see how much she needs help at this time of her young life."

In these days when May was conducting her drawing classes in Boston, she often traveled back and forth upon the train in company with Mr. French, a family friend, and the father of Daniel Chester French, who was already showing surprising artistic talent. The two discussed the youth's unusual ability and his skill with a jackknife. A grotesque figure of a frog in clothes, carved from a turnip, had greatly impressed the boy's family, and upon viewing it, Mrs. French had exclaimed, "Daniel, there is your career."

On learning of the young man's gift, May Alcott promptly offered to lend him her modeling tools, and it was a memorable evening in the French family when Dan was bidden by his father to harness the horse and bring back from the village

Miss Alcott's material. On his return the family gathered round the dining-room table, to share in an evening of modeling, Dan making a dog's head in his first attempt with the sculptor's clay. This was as crucial a moment in young French's career as was that in the life of Louisa Alcott when she was asked to write a story for young girls and answered doubtfully, "I'll try." And Mr. French's grateful memory of the friend who gave him his first lump of clay has been voiced in his charming word picture embodied in the opening pages of this book.

During this busy winter, the "book for girls" desired by Louisa's publishers did not materialize, and in the spring they again made a request for it. Then it was that she set herself the task, which in two months' time was practically completed, — that of embodying the story of her own household and youthful experiences in a volume entitled "Little Women." In July, 1868, the book was ready to go to press, and it was published in October, when its immediate success lifted, once and for all, the financial burden which up to this time had weighed heavily upon Louisa Alcott's shoulders.

She wrote in her journal, on July 15, 1868, "Have finished 'Little Women', and sent off 402 pages.

May is designing pictures for it. Hope it will go."
She little guessed how magnificently this hope was
to be realized.

In the "Amy" of "Little Women", as has been
stated, May's artistic career is truthfully depicted,
and with the proceeds of this book the elder sister
was able to gratify her ardent wish to give May
the art training in Europe which she desired.

CHAPTER IV

May and Louisa Abroad

THE crucial year 1868, which had witnessed the birth of "Little Women" and the turning of the tide in the financial fortunes of its author, closed with the completion of the sequel to the much-praised book. The second volume, like the first, was written in two months' time, and the opening of the new year, 1869, saw the manuscript delivered to the eager publishers.

The new year also witnessed a scattering of the Alcott family. Orchard House was temporarily closed, and Mr. Alcott started on a journey westward, while his wife went to visit her married daughter and May resumed her work in Boston, joining Louisa, who, with the coming of her younger sister, forsook her quiet boarding place in Brookline Street for more pretentious quarters. This change, however, failed to give the satisfaction that both desired, and in describing its drawbacks, Louisa wrote:

"May and I went to the new Bellevue Hotel in Beacon Street. She does n't enjoy quiet corners as I do, so we took a sky-parlor, and had a queer time whisking up and down in the elevator, eating in a marble café, and sleeping on a sofa-bed that we might be genteel. It did n't suit me at all. A great gale nearly blew the roof off. Steam-pipes exploded, and we went hungry. I was very tired with my hard summer, with no rest for the brains that earn the money."

This experiment not proving satisfactory, the following month they left the Bellevue and moved to rooms in Chauncy Street, there to spend the next two months before returning to Concord, where they were forced to reopen Orchard House for Mrs. Alcott, who was anxious to return to her home.

After the completion of the much-needed spring cleaning and the carrying on of household duties, summer found Louisa worn out with care and work, and much in need of rest. In July, she joined her cousins the Frothinghams, in Canada, spending a month there, at the end of which time May departed for Mount Desert, where during August she also enjoyed both rest and recreation before resuming many home responsibilities. The autumn found the whole family in Boston, Mr. and Mrs. Alcott staying with their married daughter, and the "workers", May and Louisa, pursuing their individual vocations in rooms which they had taken in Pinckney Street.

In January, 1870, Louisa suffered the loss of her voice, and her general health was so poor that it required a heroic effort to supply the persistent demands for her literary work; but despite ill health she was able to produce "An Old-Fashioned Girl", which appeared the following March.

Then, in April of this year came a long-hoped-for opportunity: a chance for the two sisters to take a European trip together. Louisa's previous taste of foreign travel had whetted her appetite for a leisurely visitation of many places from which, in the capacity of a companion for an invalid, she had obtained but scant enjoyment. Now there was an opportunity to travel without financial worry, and in the company of the cheerful and enthusiastic young sister to whom she might have the pleasure of showing the chosen spots that had most appealed to her sense of beauty.

This plan was made possible through the generosity of a friend, Miss Alice Bartlett, who invited May to take the trip with her, on the condition that Louisa should also accompany them; thus, the lucky May was as usual provided for, and the ample returns now coming from Louisa's books convinced the authoress that she could afford to allow herself a well-earned holiday across seas.

On April 2, 1870, the sisters and their friend sailed in the French steamship *Lafayette* for Brest, and on arrival took a delightful trip through France before carrying out their plan to settle in Italy for the winter, where May could profit by a sojourn in the artist's Paradise. The younger sister was as usual the life of the party, and with sketchbook in hand, eagerly embraced every chance to capture picturesque bits. They stopped at Vevay and at Bix, and the latter part of April saw them at Morlaix, where May was enraptured by gables, turrets, fountains, and churches, and was soon sketching in the town of St. Melanie, surrounded by admiring circles of small boys.

Another week found them at Dinan; there they slipped into delightful quarters at Madame Coste's pension, and though it was Good Friday when they took possession, they found themselves in a veritable realm of summer, with birds singing and flowers blooming in the fields; and from their windows the view of the beautiful valley proved a delight to all, while, to their greater satisfaction, view, birds, flowers, good food, and comfortable quarters were procured for the modest sum of a dollar a day each.

BEDROOM OF MAY AND LOUISA, DINAN, 1870
From a pen sketch by May Alcott

Of her first impressions of this stopping place
May wrote enthusiastically:

"I am in such perfect bliss that I must write
and tell you all about things here and our goings
on generally, that you may see why I am so happy.
In the first place, air soft and lovely like early
June at home. We sit with open windows and
wear spring clothes, are out the greater part of
the day, seeing such enchanting old ruins, picturesque towers and churches, and crumbling fortifications, that it seems almost like a dream, and if I
did n't see Lu admiring the landscape, I should
often doubt if I were myself. It seems impossible
that less than three weeks has transported us here,
after seeing Morlaix and doing so much beside.
This air makes me very sleepy all the time, so I
don't get up as early as I should like to; but get
dressed before coffee is brought up to us, then do
some French exercises and study verbs till ten,
when we have breakfast. Then I take my big
sketch-book and wander forth perching about
on my pretty little camp-stool Alice has given
me, whenever anything strikes me as especially
lovely.

"With the exception of ancient Rome, this town
is as old as anything we shall see, and Murray says

[73]

'affords as much for the painter's-easel and brush, as anything on the continent.' Yesterday, we went to some lovely gardens surrounding the most beautiful Gothic church, old and gray, with vines clinging about the stone ornaments and running over the great roof, almost to the top of the spire, and all this on a level with the principal part of the town, the whole being built on very high ground with fortifications and moat, which in old times made Dinan almost impregnable, but now the crumbling walls are overhung with the soft luxuriant ivy and clinging vines in all parts; even the stone archways of the town have little verdant plateaux on top, and women with immaculate caps sit about looking so picturesque that I long to make pictures on every hand."

May repeatedly expresses her joy in this life that so truly appeals to her, writing to her sister Anna:

"You ask if after dreaming of foreign parts for so many years I am not a little disappointed in the reality. But I can truly say that everything so far has been quite as picturesque, new, and lovely as I expected: and what surprises me is that so many things should be so nearly what I thought to find them."

She is impatient to reproduce the new scenes with brush and pencil, exclaiming:

"I get angry with myself for not having the power of delineating the enchanting views and objects which you would all enjoy so much. If I could only use colors easily it would all go well, but never having painted from nature, I am timid about beginning; but think I must come to it and plunge along the best I can, going on the principle of its being better to try and fail than not to try at all. I am so happy I often say to myself, 'If this be I, as I think it be, I have a little dog at home and he'll know me', to make sure it is not all dreams, and I shall wake up to find myself in my own little room at 'Apple Slump'."

At this time May sends a little sketch of their apartment, of which Louisa writes:

"May has drawn our Salon, for you, with Alice on the sofa, and me reading by the fire. It is very good, only it gives the idea of a larger room than it is. The dark oak panels are very effective, and the bird-cage in the window introduces little *Dribble* the bird, who is a funny mite and a great pet of ours. . . .

"May is well and jolly, and very good to her

crooky old sister. Alice is kind and funny, and we rub on nicely as can be. If I can only get my bones right all will be so nice and pleasant."

A few days earlier, May had sent another sketch, of which she wrote:

"Here I have sketched in the roughest way, our abiding-place for the present, just to give mother an idea of the most modern house in Dinan, from the upper window of which she will see Lu nodding at her, as that is our little Salon, furnished prettily with blue damask and looking quite homelike with our pictures and books about. I study my French every day and sketch a little, but the ruined castles, bell-towers and churches are so lovely it seems absurd to try to draw them, and I long to use color for the pretty flowers, ferns and trailing ivy running over the gray stones, all about is truly enchanting, and is nothing done with the pencil.

"I long to try painting a fine row of arches in a shadowy light that makes the effect very beautiful, but don't dare sit long in these dreadfully damp places, for when one enters from the outside air, it is like going into a refrigerator, and sends a dreadful chill to one's bones. I can't understand how old women I see kneeling on the cold stones

Notre salon chez Mndlle Coste

MADEMOISELLE COSTE'S SALON, DINAN, 1870.   LOUISA AT THE FIREPLACE

From a pen sketch by May Alcott

for hours, can stand it, though such real devotion makes an impression on me."

They remained at Dinan for two happy months, while May sketched industriously, her friend, Alice Bartlett, hunted antiques and curios, and Louisa wrote, rested, and reveled in the beauty of their surroundings. They rode about in curious donkey carts, visiting ruined châteaux and quaint villages and taking river excursions.

One of these old châteaux in particular was entertainingly described in the home letters, in which the sisters shared their doings with the family circle. It was "inhabited by a farmer who kept his hog in the great banqueting-hall, his grain in the chapel, and his hens in the lady's chamber." A picturesque old castle, with ivy climbing up the broken towers, and with it went the story of the lady of the château, who was "starved to death by her cruel brothers, and buried in the moat, where her bones were found long afterwards, and whose ghost still haunted the place."

More than one of these ruined castles had fallen from its high estate, and some were haunted by less desirable occupants than the great lady's ghost, for on a subsequent occasion the sisters, when exploring a dignified ruin, encountered a truly terrifying apparition in the guise of an infuriated sow with a family of twelve small pigs. This unlooked-for occupant charged at them so fiercely that they fled in dismay, recalling the dreadful vision of a woman whom they had once seen whose nose had been bitten off by an angry pig. Taking to their heels they flew to cover, and Louisa jumped over a hedge and pulled May after her, later describing the attacking pigs as "tall, round-backed wretches, who ran like race-horses, and were no respecter of persons."

From Tours, May sent a glowing account of their surroundings, declaring that words failed to describe the wonderful cathedral, that they occupied a most palatial apartment, and that it was all "too good to be true", although when June 21 finds them at Amboise, she interjects the comment that she finds herself fairly sated with grandeur, writing:

"I am a little tired of Castles and wish I could only visit one a month, and then I could fully appreciate them. However, the view from this one is truly perfect looking off on one side over the winding Loire with the little town beneath its high walls."

The memories of Catherine de' Medici and of the ill-fated Mary Queen of Scots kindle May's imagination, while Louisa suggests that the old stones should be able to tell wonderful tales of the scenes they had witnessed, remarking that "The Reminiscences of a Rook" might be the title for a good story, dealing with these long-lived birds which in such numbers inhabited the old towers. The viewpoints of the two sisters are interestingly contrasted in their varying descriptions, Louisa finding "stories in stones", while May only discerned numberless charming pictures.

The latter experienced special delight in the château at Chenonceaux, where everything remained just as it was when all its chambers were tenanted by kings and queens, and May declares:

"I never have enjoyed anything more in my life, and arranged my hat in Mary Queen of Scots' mirror with great satisfaction. Such tapestries and pictures as they did have, and such taste as we don't have now. I don't expect to see anything more interesting in all our travels. The long gallery of fine portraits in this curious place seemed to be alive, and the surroundings, even to the smallest things, like pen-and-ink stands, hand-mirrors, etc., used by the Queens kept up the illusion so perfectly that I began to feel a crown sprouting from my head, and ermine trailing behind me, and it was not till we were whirling along a very dusty road to the hotel, that I could bring myself to think of, or look at, anything short of royalty."

These days of recreation and wandering in Europe, with May and her companion, were perhaps the happiest in Louisa's life, for she loved the foreign scenes, reveled in freedom from family cares, and best of all was receiving a generous income from her books, which she exulted in, not for herself, but for those whose welfare was far dearer than her own.

At this time she wrote of her royalties:

"A nice letter with July account of $6,212, a neat little sum for the Alcotts, 'who can't make money'! With $10,000 well invested, and more coming in all the time, I think we may venture to enjoy ourselves, after the hard times we have had."

Two months at Dinan were followed by more wanderings and explorations of cathedrals and châteaux, and the end of June found them at Geneva, where Louisa had stayed five years before, and where she felt much at home; from there they moved in to Bex, a quiet little place among the mountains, where they enjoyed warmth and a lovely view. May, who was always ready for a strenuous outing, took an exciting trip to the pass of St. Bernard, which thoroughly appealed to her love of adventure, and regarding which she wrote at length to her family:

"I am almost afraid to begin a description of my trip to the pass of St. Bernard, but as Lu did n't go, and so cannot tell the tale, I must do my best to put before you our adventures by field and flood and fire, for really a more exciting time I never had, as we were in danger many times and even the guide thought us very courageous and plucky. Well, to begin, I must tell you that last Thursday, Lena Warren and I determined on doing the great excursion by ourselves if nobody turned up to join us, and as that did n't happen, we decided to go immediately while we had fine weather and moonlight. So we telegraphed to Martigny (an hour's ride in the cars from here) to have a carriage and the guide, Maurice, ready for us at 4 o'clock next morning, and taking our bundles, of waterproof and thick sacques, we bade our sisters an affectionate farewell, as they evidently thought we never should return, and that it was the height of rashness to attempt a three days' trip alone.

"However, we felt sure, after studying Murray

carefully, and finding out all particulars from a Polish gentleman here who had just returned from the Pass, that we could do it. So we turned our backs upon our friends and went at nine o'clock P.M. to Martigny finding our room ready at the hotel and tumbled directly into bed for a four hours' sleep, as we were to be called so early. Then before sunrise we were up, had coffee, and mounted our open barouche with a nice man to drive and guide, and rode through the loveliest valley and along the most turbulent little river, for eight hours till we stopped at a little town, for some refreshments, and to rest the mule, then having been gradually ascending all the way we now began to wind along the edge of a fearful precipice, but the road was so perfect that I was continually wondering how they ever built such a one on the straight edge of the mountains. We kept meeting loads of tourists all in gay costumes with Alpenstocks, and the general bowing and *bon-jouring* seemed so friendly and sociable that, though it had now begun to rain and the cover of our carriage was buttoned down, yet our spirits rose higher and higher until we reached the Cantine (as they call the place for leaving the vehicles and mounting mules).

"We were ready for anything, and lucky for us

that we were, for things looked a little dubious. The rain poured in torrents, and it now being about 4 o'clock P.M. we might either spend the night in this horrid little house already filled with people caught in the rain, and afraid to go on, or boldly plunge along in the storm, climbing for two hours to reach the Hospice. We persuaded the guide to take us along, and Lena mounted the mule, while I, in my waterproof with thick boots and my sun umbrella over me, marched up and up, plowing through the mud and wading the river (which had burst all bounds and carried away the road in places) up to my knees in the ice-cold water. The lightning flashed and the tremendous claps of thunder seemed so near us, that the mule stopped and could n't be persuaded to go on, till a hard beating and yanking obliged him not only to start again, but to carry us through several places where the water came up to his belly, and a false step would have sent us over a fall in one place, and been certain death.

"All this I really enjoyed intensely and began to think I was a little courageous, when the guide told me he had never been in such a storm on the mountains before, as the thunder was always so near the peaks that people were often killed by lightning, and it was considered dangerous, very dangerous to travel these mountain passes at such times. My heart sank within me, my clothes clung to me so that it was like dragging a leaden weight after me every step I took. Ladies all ride up from the Cantine, and Lena, like the rest, took her mule, and though very wet, having no waterproof, was saved the immense exertion of the very steep climb in soaking garments. One can never calculate about the weather here, as it often rains on the mountains when perfectly clear below, and when we left Martigny a more lovely morning I never saw, not a cloud in the sky, and we hardly expected a tempest a few hours later. But I would n't have missed seeing the mountains in the storm, for it was more fearfully beautiful than anything I ever imagined.

"At last thoroughly wet to our skins, we reached the Hospice, where a handsome, kindly Priest met us and conducted us to a room with two pretty curtained beds in it, and a grated window looking on the lake and towards Italy. A woman appeared, and helped us off with our clothes, which stuck tightly to us, being so wet, and brought us plain warm flannels, peasant's dresses and underclothes. These we put on with rapture, being chilled with the cold air of the immense stone building. It was hard to find any skirt long enough for me, and we had great fun arranging one skirt over another in a kind of over-dress, and then my velvet jacket to cover up the waist, and putting on a pair of cloth slippers the size of mud-scows, my toilet was finished.

"We descended to the *salle-à-manger* where our handsome Priest awaited us and complimented us immensely on our having accomplished such a feat; then seating us before an immense open fire, with an old English lady, who spends her summers there, we all sat around and talked and warmed ourselves till tea was served for our benefit, and a delicious dinner followed. Fine pictures hung about, presents from different visitors, and a piano from the Prince of Wales stood in a corner. The priests charge nothing for food and lodgings, but people leave what they choose behind them, and some tourists are very mean, slinking away without giving anything after receiving the lordly hospitality of the devoted brotherhood. From all the numbers at the Cantine, none dared the storm but three Englishwomen and ourselves, all the gentlemen who started up, turned back in fear of the storm.

"The priest, for there is only one who sees and entertains the thousands of visitors who come every year, told us a great deal about how the Hospice was carried on, and the adventures he had had in the eleven years he had been there, through summer and winter. Beside the average 13,000 tourists that visit the establishment, they rescue from the snow and storms great numbers of peasants yearly. They know what ladies need up there, for on going to our room we found the beds had been warmed that we might not take cold, every comfort was provided for us, and I never slept more delightfully than I did there after all our adventures, and knowing also that we were only separated by a little grating from a host of priests. At five next morning we were up to hear service in the chapel and I enjoyed the unific very much, as I always do in these Catholic churches. On going out for a clamber on the rocks, we were startled by a tremendous howling and baying and suddenly out from a kind of cellar rushed six or seven great dogs, who all bounded towards us licking our hands and smelling to see if we were hurt. They had the most human eyes I ever saw and I could well imagine their wonderful feats in the winter when they rescue so many travelers from the snow, for they are very powerfully built and look immensely strong though so affectionate and gentle. I was glad to have seen the real St. Bernard dogs, and quite proud to have them slobber over and caress me.

"We walked into Italy, which was an operation of ten minutes only, and I should have liked to have gone down on the Italian side. . . . We saw the lovely lakes close to the Hospice, and snow surrounded us everywhere, and we picked up some of the immense hail-stones which fell the night before. After a good hot breakfast we were shown photographs and various souvenirs which visitors like to carry away with them, and I bought several. We left a large piece of gold in the chapel and gave a good bit to each waiter, then bade our friends good-bye, and trotted down the mountain in the clear bracing air, and could hardly believe with our thick coats on we should find it scorching hot in the town below. Our guide followed with the mule and bundles, and on my way I picked some Alpine flowers to press for mother. We could hardly realize that the way which seemed so easy in the sunlight, could have been so fearfully difficult the night before, for the roaring river had diminished to a brook, and everything seemed peaceful and perfectly grand. I much preferred the wild stormy scene and blessed my stars that everything had happened as it did."

At this time, the breaking out of the Franco-Prussian War found an echo in the home letters, and the Alcott family, whose anxiety was beginning to be aroused, were reassured by the travelers that Switzerland was an absolutely safe stopping place, and they were charged not to grow uneasy if foreign mails were delayed.

Throngs of visitors were then seeking refuge in Switzerland, and the suppression of newspapers by government orders cut off the sojourners from all but the vaguest reports, and left them in considerable uncertainty as to their future plans. But August found them at Vevay, settled at a comfortable pension, where the gay season was in full blast, despite the war, and the travelers wrote of the presence there of the ex-queen of Spain and her family, also of Don Carlos, the rightful heir to the Spanish throne.

Reports of the defeat of the French in two battles seemed to give Louisa some satisfaction, as she wrote to her family, "I side with the Prussians, for they sympathized with us in our war. Hooray for old Pruss."

During that August stay at Vevay, Louisa and May spent many restful days among the hills, and the former's health improved so much that she was able to take five-mile tramps and to sleep twelve hours at a stretch, an accomplishment seldom attained by her. One may picture the sisters in company with other friends driving up in a big landeau to the picturesque chalet of M. Nicaud, the owner of their pension, to be regaled with a "tip-top Swiss dinner", and entertained by a view from this farm perched high among the hills, sitting on rustic seats and peering out through drifting fog and summer showers, to catch the fleeting glimpses of the landscape below them, and finally tramping home late in the evening over muddy roads. Such an achievement for Louisa betokened a return to her old-time robust health, which, had she spared herself in later years, might have once more been hers; but she was born to consume every ounce of vital energy in her determination to secure everything in her power for those she loved.

While they remained at Vevay, the war news became more and more thrilling, and the Alcott daughters felt that it was not wise to linger, so they prepared to cross the Alps, bound for Milan and the lakes. Paris had been bombarded and Vevay was crowded with refugees from that city, and from Strasbourg. Meanwhile, Louisa and May, who had determined to make the most of their opportunities to master French, worked at their lessons with an obliging teacher whom they had found. In this endeavor to concentrate upon their studies, May seems to have succeeded best, for her sister found the process too exhausting, and gave up the task, exclaiming that she "never could study", adding, "the little brains I have left I want to keep for future works, and not exhaust them on grammar — the invention of Satan."

October, 1870, found them at Lake Como, where the charm and beauty of their surroundings brought compensation for those years of drudgery which had at last ended in this release from household burdens and financial cares.

Of their trip into Italy May wrote enthusiastically:

DEAREST MOTHER: I want to write you a circumstantial account of our triumphal entry into Italy over the Simplon Pass.

From Vevay past the dear old Castle of Chillon standing out in the water, gray and solemn in the early light, by our old friend the white-capped Dent de Midi and up the lovely valley of the Rhone is something to remember . . .

All the party were up at four the next morning and, lighted by lanterns, for it was pitch dark, we were surrounded by our own luggage and waited patiently until it was announced that there were no places in either of the immense diligences which stood before us ready to start immediately. This

was enough to dampen the ardor of a less gay
crowd than ours, but we fell upon the official and
smiled to such an extent that he suddenly ordered
out a calèche with two horses and a superb driver
dressed in a red coat, cocked hat with gold lace
and yellow small clothes, who whirled us out of
the square, and then though it was still starlight,
we began the steady ascent.

The air grew colder and colder, till at last having
plied the bottle many times in vain, I got out and
walked to warm myself. The other two remained
in the carriage wrapped up to such an extent that
only eyes were visible, and the sketch I took looks
like a portrait of Egyptian women. They hardly
dared uncover their hands enough to eat a bit of
chicken with comfort for fear of a nipped finger
and it was funny to see the horses covered with a
little hoar frost. I tingled when Monte Rosa
opened before us with its dazzling white snow
against a perfectly clear blue sky and behind us the
Bernese Alps and the glaciers. This was something
to have lived for. . . .

We had a miserable dinner at Simplon and then
I nearly stood on my head with delight at the
intense beauty of the valley of Garda for anything
wilder and more picturesque cannot be imagined.
Then this wonderful road which we had traversed

so far in safety led along the edge of precipices, through tunnels and over cataracts to such an exciting extent, that nothing short of the little farce which was now to be enacted could have taken my attention off the magnificent scenery about us. At Iselle our baggage was to be examined and passports demanded, but I not having one of the latter, was to play the part of ladies'-maid, so out came my earrings, up went my curls and tying a veil over my rather dressy hat and throwing a waterproof over my new travelling dress I dismounted to help the ladies out and arrange the cloaks and bundles, then stood quietly one side hoping the sharp-eyed officials would overlook me. They did n't, however, and after examining every parcel in the carriage looking at me from head to foot as if taking an inventory of all my clothing, and thoroughly overhauling all the trunks, we were allowed after great deliberation to continue our descent through this enchanting valley, everything growing more and more Italian in appearance till we entered Domo L'Ossola by sunset and from there drove to Stresa by moonlight. This I consider making a Pass successfully, for it is not every traveler who sees sunrise in the Alps, an Italian sunset and first sight of Lago Maggiore by moonlight, all in one day.

At two o'clock, we took the steamboat to Luini and here among the jeers and shouts of an Italian crowd, Alice and I mounted to the very top of a very high diligence and sat with perfect complacency amid the baggage, while Louisa from the coupé begged us to come down and the inside passengers craned their necks to see of what nation the insane travelers could be, who preferred to view the landscape from that great elevation. But I wouldn't have missed the enjoyment of the next few hours for all the ridicule in the world and the beauty of that drive from Luini to Lugano can hardly be overrated.

We drove into Lugano by moonlight with our superb cocher playing a festive tune on his Robin Hood's horn which hung by gilt bands at his side, putting on two brakes, driving four horses and making himself agreeable to us all at the same time. I consider this man a person of mind, for he spoke three languages easily and did everything with such a superior air that I felt intensely honored to have him lift me down in his great arms when we reached the Hotel Washington. As a very proper ending to this delightful day Lu and myself can only say that we went to the opera in our robes-de-nuit, for from the window of our palatial apartment we looked directly on to the stage and behind the scenes of the theatre on the opposite side of a very narrow alley, and heard the last two acts of *Traviata* finely sung. It reminded me so much of the old days, when Annie, dressed up in the velvet puffs and everlasting top-boots, sang baritone to Lu's soprano and brought down the house in every act.

Of this same dramatic evening Louisa wrote to her sister Nan:

"As if a heavenly lake under our windows with moonlight *ad libitum* was not enough, we had music next door, and on leaning out of a little back window, we made the splendid discovery that we could look on the stage of the opera house across a little alley. . . . With what rapture I stared at the scenes going on below me, as I stood there wrapped in my yellow bed-quilt, and saw gallant knights in armor warble sweetly to plump ladies in masks, or pretty peasants fly wildly from ardent lovers in red tights; also a dishevelled maid who tore her hair in a forest, while a man aloft made thunder and lightning, — and I *saw him do it*. It was the climax to a splendid day, for few travellers can go to the opera luxuriously in their night-gowns and take naps between the acts as I did."

What an enlightening glimpse of the submerged Louisa Alcott, that fun-adoring, freedom-loving creature who was for over half a century cribbed, cabined, and confined by her New England conscience in her New England habitations. One is at this point tempted to inquire, Might not her brilliant literary gift have blossomed vividly and even luxuriantly could she have had, not days, but years of leisure and emancipation in an environment as lovely and inspiring as this described by her, with gay attire, moonlight on balconies, fine music floating from the throats of prima donnas in filmy robes, and gallant knights in armor? But it was not to be. The moving finger wrote but seven magic letters, and they spelled CONCORD.

Louisa Alcott's pen was destined to keep alive not great, romantic, or historic personages, but vivid little people of New England, and not all the allurement of the Old World could have drawn her from her home life of sacrifice. May could escape from her New England heritage, but not Louisa. Yet it is good to think of her, if only for a single night, wrapped in a yellow bedquilt, staring with "rapture" at gallant knights, and hearing them "warble to plump ladies", while the stage thunder crashed and the philosophy of Concord was forgot.

A sail upon the magic lake, a trip by carriage to Menaggio, and then to Cadenabbia by boat, and on to Milan a few days later, where May joined a young artist friend with whom she eagerly discussed plans for profiting by the free art schools at Milan, Naples, and Florence, a prospect which truly delighted both sisters.

In Florence they were greeted by many friends, and had numerous opportunities to enter into the social life there, regarding which May wrote at the end of October:

"Last night we went to a party made for us at the house of the sculptor Ball, who with his wife called on us immediately on our arrival, saying they had been expecting us, and looking forward with great pleasure to doing the honors of Florence to us. We returned their call and saw Mr. Ball in his fine studio among his marbles, — all lovely but none so strong and full of power as his Washington, in the Boston Public Garden. He has never seen it since it was finished in bronze; and was pleasantly surprised by the unanimous approbation it has met with from critical Boston.

"Mr. Powers and Mr. Hart, besides several other sculptors and artists were introduced to us, and invited us to their studios. It seems 'Little Women' is as well known here as in Boston, and has made many friends for Louisa. She was showered with compliments from the distinguished people here, among whom was our Minister, Mr. Marsh, (who is a literary man himself); also Miss Foley the cameo-cutter, and several ladies from Rome, who will return there in a few weeks, and were full of kind offers about apartments, etc. Mr. Gould was not there, and we hear that he and his wife go into society very little, however, we mean to see him at his studio if it is possible. Mr. Hart, who is a gray haired beau, but quite devoted to me, begs me to take a corner of his studio and model a bust, or little head, of Lu. But as everything seems uncertain about the climate suiting the invalids, I don't dare begin anything, and devote myself to sight-seeing and studying the fine pictures."

November found them at last in the Eternal City, towards which all roads that they had traversed had been tending. Meanwhile, they had journeyed across the Alps by moonlight, and had spent ideal days at Parma, Pisa, Bologna, and Florence. Some things proved disappointing, but Nature never, save when the cold winds blew, and sunny Italy withheld its sunshine. Louisa found some pictures "faded" and some rooms "very damp", and they were glad to purchase furs in Florence;

and when at last they found themselves in Rome, a dismal rain was falling and the impressions of the elder sister, who suffered from the dampness, were not inspiriting. She wrote:

"I felt as if I had been there before and knew all about it. Always oppressed by a sense of sin, dirt, and general decay of all things. Not well, so saw things through blue glasses. May in bliss with lessons, sketching and her dreams."

May's dreams were surely coming true, even as she had unswervingly believed they would from the beginning: the life abroad which she had longed for, the opportunity to study art, which was her heart's desire, was being realized, — nothing could keep her from her own; and her beloved Louisa, clever and famous, of whose increasing reputation she was perchance at times just a bit jealous, because she felt convinced that she had also received from heaven as great a gift, which she was soon to demonstrate, — Louisa was here to share her wondrous opportunities, and at the same time, as she hoped, to win back health and strength.

But they had happened on an inauspicious season, for clouds obscured the sunshine, and the persistent rains did much to dampen their pleasures, although their quarters were dry and comfortable. Their apartment in the Piazza Barbarini was warm and cozy, and they thanked Heaven for it, as it rained for two months almost incessantly, and Rome was fairly inundated.

Then while the clouds still threatened, the gloom was deepened by sad news from America, which told them of the death of their brother-in-law, John Pratt, to whom both sisters were deeply attached. To their own sorrow and sense of loss was added the weight of their sympathy for the bereaved sister so far away, who was now left without support or a strong arm on which to lean. At once Louisa's stern conscience bade her take up her idle pen on behalf of the children of her much beloved brother-in-law, who must be properly provided for. Early in 1871, she began work on "Little Men", which was completed in time for summer publication. In the meantime, it was decided that May must not relinquish her art work, but must continue to pursue her studies.

Plans were discussed and finances computed, and then Louisa decided that she must return home in the spring, but that May should remain for a year longer, in order to complete her lessons; she must be free and happy to cultivate her talent. Concord was calling to Louisa, but not to May; she should be left in London, under her lucky star.

After spending the month of March at Albano, where May did many sketches and won admiring glances from the officers from Turin, they moved to Venice and then on to London, where they went into lodgings at Brompton Road. They spent the month of May there, finding a group of friends known previously to Louisa, who took much pleasure in introducing her younger sister, to whom she had the joy of showing her favorite haunts in London. It was arranged that May should begin lessons with Rowbotham, a prominent teacher, and ere long she had settled down to work, while her sister made plans for her trip homeward, and their friend, Alice Bartlett, with whom they had spent a happy year, took leave of them.

In June, Louisa sailed away to face a harrowing experience on the home passage, for smallpox broke out among the passengers, and her roommate was stricken with it, so that she thought daily she might herself be the next victim. Happily she escaped the infection, and after twelve anxious days she landed, to find her father waiting for her with the cheering news that "Little Men" was out, and that fifty thousand copies had been sold before publication.

Throughout the summer, May's letters told of her pleasant life in London, and of her interest in making highly commended copies of Turner. But as autumn approached, it became evident that she was much needed at home, where Louisa's strength was being too severely tested. Marmee was feeble, and Nan very sorrowful, while her boys needed a strong hand. Moreover, May's eyes were suffering from over use, and it seemed best that she should temporarily relinquish her art work in London.

She came back on November 19, 1871, happy and full of helpful plans for all the family, bringing into the household her much-needed sunny and vital personality.

How they responded to her merry tales of small adventures, and with what speed regained their cheerfulness, as they admired her paintings, studied her portfolio of sketches, and listened to tales of her numerous admirers; for May seemed always to have a circle of devoted swains ready to do her bidding at all times, and in every place, were it Concord or London.

It was a special joy to have her again with them, when they gathered at the Pratt farm upon Thanksgiving day, to help dispel the sad thoughts of their recent bereavement. And on November 29th they joined in celebrating the double birthday of Louisa (thirty-nine), and of her father (seventy-two), a day marked by general contentment, for there were no financial worries; two maids had been secured to do the household work, and the author of "Little Women" had announced from her Boston retreat that she was better both in mind and body, declaring:

"All goes well at home, with May to run the machine in her cheery, energetic style, and amuse Marmee and Nan with gay histories. Had a furnace put in, and all enjoyed the new climate. No more rheumatic fevers and colds, with picturesque open-fires. Mother is to be cozy if money can do it. She seems to be now, and my long-cherished dream has come true, for she sits in a pleasant room, with no work, no care, no poverty to worry, but peace and comfort all about her, and children glad and able to stand between trouble and her. Thank the Lord! I like to stop and remember my mercies. Working and waiting for them makes them very welcome."

CHAPTER V

London in 1873

At forty, Louisa Alcott's resolve to make her family independent financially had been accomplished, but it still remained for her to realize her dream of giving her younger sister sufficient opportunity for the development of her artistic talent. She had recalled May from her work in London in 1871, to share in the household responsibilities, and two years later she sent her again to Europe to resume her interrupted studies.

The winter previous had been a trying one for all concerned. Anna had been desperately ill with pneumonia, and it was only after weeks of patient nursing by her sisters that she gradually crawled back to health. During her convalescence, Louisa, who had taken refuge in Boston in order to finish her forthcoming book, entitled "Work", returned home to take May's place, insisting that after this long period of nursing she should go back to the art studies, which she had been forced to relinquish. Then, as the spring advanced, she packed May off for Europe, with a present of one thousand dollars, to enable her to continue her work in London.

May sailed for England on April 26, 1873, happy

and hopeful, once more to take up her brush and pencil under the best instructors. Soon her home letters were filled with entertaining accounts of her surroundings, and of the progress that she was making in her work. She wrote enthusiastically from London, two months later:

"Most truly might I, like the little vagabond in the song, end each of these lovely June days with the refrain, 'Oh, who so contented as I!' For can it be otherwise with me in this wonderful city, where an industrious art student finds such an endless amount to see, study and enjoy, that the only difficulty is to decide where to begin.

"On this my second visit after an interval of a year and a half, I am more convinced than ever that nowhere can a young artist, man or woman, live so cheaply and comfortably and study under such favorable circumstances as in London. . . .

"Arrived here armed with an address or two, it is an easy matter to find excellent board in the neighborhood of the galleries. I have a large airy room on the second floor, well furnished, with long windows opening on to a balcony which overlooks one of the prettiest squares in the city. The use of a handsome drawing-room is mine also.

"The table is good, though not laden with the

great variety we have at home; and I find the simple solid fare much more healthful than the lavish mixture in America. Such joints of beef, such legs of mutton I never enjoyed before. One or two sorts of vegetables, a simple pudding or tart, good Stilton cheese, and the best ale, make up the meal, to which I do justice I assure you after six hours of painting.

"All these comforts can be had for thirty shillings a week, about seven dollars in gold.

"Added to this is another advantage which my artistic sisters will appreciate as I do. Shops abound with cheap clothing of all sorts ready made. Work is also so cheap that a young woman of moderate means can get up a neat and handsome wardrobe for half the sum it costs at home. By waiting till August, when the fashionable season is over, one can buy charming things for a mere song, and get dresses made for a few dollars. But the crowning glory of all to the newcomer is the fine galleries and exhibitions to be enjoyed.

"First the National, in my humble opinion the best in the world, with its twelve large rooms full of originals from the Dutch, Italian, and Spanish and English schools; two of the latter devoted to Turner's oils, while below is an exquisite collection of water-colors by him, to be seen for the asking.

One also has the right to copy two days in the week (when the public are excluded) any picture in the room, by merely making an application to the superintendent, Mr. Norman.

"Next comes the Kensington Museum, a beautiful building, with its numberless immense halls of curiosities, and a great collection of pictures from all schools. Here also are some of Turner's best, and two rooms of his studies in sepia, and unfinished water-colors, are most interesting and profitable showing his conscientious way of working even the most minute detail. Particularly noticeable is this in a bird's-eye-view of Rome, not larger than half a carte-de-visite, with its numberless domes, roofs and steeples so correctly drawn, and exquisitely colored, that it made me dizzy to think of the time and pains he must have spent on it.

"Here one is free to copy three days in the week. There is also a school in connection with the museum, where the instruction is good and the course a very thorough one, being the same as that in the School of Design in Boston, while under the charge of Mr. Salisbury Tuckerman, whose great ability and correctness in his work will long be gratefully remembered by those who were so fortunate as to be his pupils.

"There can be no more thorough grounding than this, beginning with simple outlines, where the great importance is felt of the purity of a line and the perfection of a curve. From the most difficult of intricate figures, to be copied entirely by the eye, one passes to flat studies, then to the round, and from pencil and chalks to colors and the life model."

After touching upon Bethnal Green, the Royal Academy, and the International, where pictures may be studied, she speaks gratefully of the privilege of sketching in Westminster Abbey, and of America's failure to furnish the poor with opportunities to enjoy art treasures, such as they enjoy abroad. She repeatedly dwells upon her pet project, that of supplying art opportunities to the people in her own country. And in referring to the enthusiasm of even the urchins in Italy for a great Madonna, she asserts:

"Ragged, dirty, picturesque, and absorbed, there they stood criticising the great picture with an enthusiasm and audacity beautiful to behold. It is easy to see that this constant opportunity for studying the best in sculpture and painting does much to educate and refine. I was greatly amused and often astonished, while sketching in France and

Italy, to hear how the little peasants crowding round my camp-stool, in talking to one another, almost invariably hit upon the best points in my sketch, or found fault with bad lines in the old church ruin, or gabled house I was drawing. They saw at once if I were getting a good copy, and congratulated me on it with smiles and nods. It seemed to be the crowning honor and joy of life to be put into a sketch themselves.

"Often in looking about me here, I feel ashamed and impatient that we, who give so generously to many good causes and spend so lavishly in many foolish ways, are so slow to move in the direction of art, for we need just the culture that alone gives. I want a really good collection of the best pictures which shall be open to all; not merely to artists, or those who can pay their fifty cents for an hour's lounge, but absolutely free, like great galleries abroad, where any beggar may solace himself with beauty, if so inclined. When we get this, and schools such as we find here, then we need not run away from home and roam about gathering up the advantages of the Old World.

"Nevertheless art life abroad is very charming and after my day among the Turners, I heartily enjoy wandering through London, taking a trip to Hampton Court, Kew, or Richmond, a row on the river, a brisk canter in the park, or a ten-mile tramp to see the May-Pole Inn. So free, so busy, so happy am I that I envy no one, and find life infinitely rich and full. Such being the case, and this my second trial of the experiment succeeding even better than the first, I feel that I may venture to say to any other young woman of moderate means, and artist longings, 'Take heart, come over and try art-life in London'."

It was while making copies of Turner's paintings at the National Gallery that May made the acquaintance of John Ruskin, who followed with great interest those studying the work of the great master of landscape painting, to whom he had accorded such lifelong praise and study. He was at once struck with the admirable copies produced by the American girl from Concord, and highly commended her productions. While it is difficult to secure any exact data concerning this brief association with Ruskin, it was recorded in the newspaper correspondence of Moncure D. Conway, a close friend of the Alcotts, who was then making his home in England, and it is stated on good authority that May Alcott's copies of Turner were given to students to study in the South Kensington Museum.

May's great enthusiasm for Turner, which no doubt at the start could be traced to the influence of Hunt, her early teacher, himself a Turner enthusiast, must have awakened a responsive chord in Ruskin's breast, as he hailed with delight those who truly appreciated the masterpieces of him who practically introduced landscape painting into England. There, to his day and generation, Ruskin had demonstrated that Turner, whose work so many of his contemporaries had thought unnatural and absurd, was in fact quite as true to nature as that of any landscape artist who had ever lived. And thus by word of mouth, and upon printed page, Ruskin effected a revolution, not only in the field of art criticism, but also in that of art production.

As one recalls the many admirable copies of Turner which May Alcott produced, it is worth while to suggest that these, and all truly fine copies of this master's work, are, as time passes, likely to hold permanent places in the great art collections, if only because so much of Turner's work is gradually fading out. Some of his finest pictures are now almost obliterated, and it is feared that at no very distant date, a large number of his great pictures will have disappeared.

The reason for this calamity has been accounted

for in several ways: in part because of the bad
pigments that Turner used at times; again because
of the careless way in which he left many pictures exposed to the glare of the sun; and also
because he sometimes mixed oil with water color.

Thus, despite the enormous amount of work
accomplished by him, so much of which is in the
English galleries to-day, it is a question how much
posterity may be enabled to enjoy. The quantity
of his production stands an unrivaled achievement
in the field of art, for he left twenty-one thousand
pictures, drawings, and sketches to testify to his
unceasing industry. This meant a picture, or a
sketch, for every one of his working days, which
output may be contrasted with the two thousand
works produced by Rubens and the four hundred
left by Rembrandt.

From time to time, May Alcott's descriptions of
her London doings found their way into print, and
the following sketch, entitled "How We Saw the
Shah", is a characteristic production:

"On a lovely June day, it was announced that
our 'carriage stopped the way.' Five happy souls
soon filled it. With many wishes for a pleasant
trip, in four different languages, from gentlemen of
four nationalities on our balcony, we drove away

for a visit to Kew Gardens. Much impressed with the elegance of our turnout, for the coachman was a stately being in gold lace, white tie, top boots etc., we drove through the Marble Arch into the Park, and found ourselves surrounded on all sides by an expectant crowd.

"Our 'Yellow Plush' condescended to inform us that the 'Shay', as he pronounced it, was going to Richmond in a royal barge, and the people were waiting for him, as he must pass this way on his road from Buckingham Palace.

"Having expressed an utter contempt for his august highness, especially his morals and manners, we decided that it was not consistent to wait for him; but as he would probably overtake us, we could then honor him with a casual glance.

"In this lofty frame of mind we rolled on, passing fine drags with gentlemen driving four-in-hand, coaches with outriders, ladies in phaetons, and whole families looking very domestic and happy in small omnibuses.

"By the Albert Memorial, with its Byzantine shaft and finely sculptured marble base, by Kensington Gardens, haunted to my fancy by Trollope, Thackeray, and Dickens's heroes and heroines, through the great gates we went, and came into the more countrylike region of Hammersmith.

"Still flocks of people lined the road. Every balcony was full, and all high steps and walls swarmed with men and boys. So eager were they to see *something* that every head was turned as we drove by, and judging from their remarks, many were firmly persuaded that my companion, who occupied the seat of honor shrouded in blue veil, was the only wife of the 'Shay' not sent back to Persia in disgrace for wanting to see and join in the festivities at Moscow.

"At last our cry of 'Sister Ann, Sister Ann, do you see anything coming?' was answered by my opposite neighbor, who commanded a fine view of the road behind us. 'I see the glitter of the Queen's Horse Guards, many carriages and much dust.'

"At this, our indifference changed suddenly to interest, for there *is* something rather exciting in the approach of royalty, even if it be only a half-savage Persian, with more diamonds than democracy. . . .

"Soon gilded helmets adorned with long horse-tails, the glittering lances and gay uniforms of the guard appeared, and flashed by, followed by eight state carriages, so shut up that little could be seen of the golden idols within. At last came the vehicle on which all eyes were fixed; but great was the disappointment, for all that could be seen were

[113]

glimpses of a dark face, with fine eyes surmounted by a hat that looked like a muff set on end, with some very brilliant ornament in front. Then came more carriages with gold-laced beings inside, more gay guards in clouds of dust, and we had seen the Shay!

"It was all over in such a minute that I hardly knew what he was like; still there is an infinite satisfaction in the thought that I can truly say in answer to the one question now asked by everybody all over England 'Have you seen the Shah?' 'Yes, I have; and I did not pay anything for the spectacle either.'

"Congratulating ourselves upon this piece of luck, we left the great road and taking to the pretty lanes, came at length to the bridge crossing the Thames, at Kew.

"A livelier sight can hardly be imagined for all the world was abroad. The river-banks were lined with gaily dressed people, and the water covered with boats of every sort, great pleasure barges, small steamers, canal-boats tugged along by used-up horses, club-boats with their eight oars, keeping perfect time, and such inviting shells that I could not resist the temptation that then and there beset me.

"As the carriage stopped near the bank, I turned

to my English friends and invited them to take a row with me. Ignoring a slight hesitancy on their part in accepting the proposal, I headed the procession, and marching up to an old boatman, asked, pointing to a captivating little craft floating below, if I could have it for an hour.

" 'It won't hold but three, and is very cranky, so if the ladies are nervous, I'd rather row you in a bigger boat,' replied the bare-legged patriarch.

"Then it was that the full audacity of my project dawned upon the party, for having explained that I proposed being skipper, coxswain, oarsman, all in one, horror fell upon all my friends. With the utmost politeness they explained that though ladies rowed in England, it was always in the chaste seclusion of 'Papa's grounds', or some more retired portion of the river than that now before us.

"But the boating fever was on me, and I could no more keep from the water than a Newfoundland dog. With a naughty satisfaction in asserting my Yankee independence, I boldly replied to their gentle hints and kindly advice:

" 'Very well: if you don't like to go, I'll go alone, for a row in the Rose I must have, in remembrance of my own boat and the quiet river at home.'

"Resolutely stepping in, and feathering my oars

in my most scientific manner, I pulled vigorously up the stream, with the true Harvard stroke, as nearly as one of the uninitiated can hope to come to it.

"Was n't it lovely? And did n't I enjoy the exercise? For after weeks of painting, my arms positively reveled in a sturdy pull, and got it too, as the current was strong and all England looking on. Yes, utterly regardless of the chaff of the boys, the dismay of my lady friends, and the amusement of gentlemen ditto, I heartily enjoyed the brief trip. I longed to stop and book some of the lovely pictures up and down the river, — the gray stone arches of the bridge, the gay crowds on the one bank, the great trees and pagoda of the garden on the other, and all the water dappled with soft shadows and green glimmers as I floated near the shore."

This sprightly picture of a London outing is very characteristic of the youngest Alcott daughter, suggesting vividly her ever-ready enjoyment of the athletic, as well as the artistic, spectacles about her, for while she pulled the "Harvard stroke" she was composing delightful sketches of the Thames, and to her satisfaction, was shocking her conventional companions.

Her progress in her work was a keen source of pleasure to Louisa, who took much pride in her accomplishments, writing concerning them:

"May still in London painting Turners, and doing pretty panels as 'pot boilers.' They sell well, and she is a thrifty child. Very happy in her success; for she has proved her talent. She has begun to copy Nature, and done well. Lovely sketches of the cloisters in Westminster Abbey, and other charming things."

During this year abroad, May worked untiringly, and besides her more serious productions, was able to produce the "pot boilers" above referred to by her sister. Then in March, 1874, her year being ended, she sailed for home with her portfolios filled with examples of her work, testifying to her months of conscientious study.

The Orchard House, which had been closed, was now reopened, put in excellent condition by May and Louisa, and decorated with many of the former's pictures. When finally the household was once more settled, Louisa, sadly in need of rest, took her departure for Boston, leaving her sister to assume the family responsibilities.

In October, Louisa engaged two pleasant rooms at the Hotel Bellevue, one of which May was to use for the classes which she was planning to conduct. There, in apartments more to their taste than the original sky parlor which they had occupied a decade earlier, they spent a busy winter, each sister successfully pursuing her chosen vocation, although Louisa was handicapped by much ill health, which made it difficult for her to furnish the copy which publishers and editors continually demanded.

"The golden goose can sell her eggs for a good price," she exclaimed at this time, "if she is n't killed by too much driving."

An example of May's artistic work produced about this time still hangs on the wall in the home of Emerson. It is a panel, such as won great popularity in the seventies, and is decorated with a spray of goldenrod and asters. Sent as a Christmas gift to Emerson, in 1874, it evoked the following note of appreciation: —

MY DEAR MAY, — I found on my return home after Christmas that the kindest and skilfulest of hands had adorned, or shall I say, lighted my study with the panel of the golden-rod and asters. It is charming to the eyes of those who cannot appreciate painting, as well as of those who can. How good and helpful and universal, therefore,

A VILLA IN FRANCE
From a pen drawing by May Alcott

the benefit which I can only begin to praise today because it will go on praising itself from day to day, and year to year, to all beholders. I value it highly, and I shall thank you silently so long as I can see.

Affectionately,
R. W. EMERSON

The following Christmas May sent a picture to Mrs. Emerson that she believed would harmonize with the colors of her room. The gift brought forth the following note:

Christmas, 1875.

Kindest thanks, my dear May, for the lovely picture in its unique and very beautiful frame. You are very thoughtful to consider the colours of my room, — the only colours I feel quite at home with. I shall place your gift over my writing-table over Clytie, and under my madonna,

Gratefully yours,
LYDIA EMERSON.

In June, 1875, one of May Alcott's dreams was realized in the opening of an Art Center in Concord. As previously suggested in her letters from Europe, she had long cherished the desire to bring to her own country and community those opportunities which she felt must foster the love of art; this she believed to be an educational force that played a vital part in the life of those across seas, who with so much less money to expend, seemed to possess so much more of the joy of living, because of the opportunities so freely offered them in the art world.

A brief account of the new project is recorded in a newspaper letter, written at this time by a Concord enthusiast, who tells of the new Studio recently opened in the town for the purpose of drawing together those wishing to cultivate a taste for art.

"The room is upon the second story of a brick building facing the Common, and was formerly used for a Masonic Hall. There are eight windows, all having blinds and shutters, which enable us to arrange the light always satisfactorily. At one end of the room is a dais, which is a foot or two above the floor and overhung by an imposing red canopy and Latin motto left there by the Masons, and upon the other sides of the room are smaller platforms upon which imaginary models have already been placed. In all respects the room is admirably adapted for a Studio. Desks and tables are placed about the room, and easels for the more ambitious of us. There are several casts hung about, and two or three portfolios filled with all sorts of good patterns from the simple effective pencil sketches of Veutin, to the water-color copies from Crowninshield, are placed there for our use. Among the collections are several pieces by Madam Theresa Higg, the remarkable flower-painter of Vevay. So you see we have enough to start with."

The writer continues:

"About fifteen of us are vastly enthusiastic about this room, which outsiders, who 'could n't draw a horse or a cow,' laughingly style the *Art Academy*. Singularly, people who cannot draw always select the most difficult of all the animal creation as the objects they 'could n't even draw.' We meet two or three times a week *en masse*, or in small detachments to work together; but the Studio being a novelty, only two weeks old, nothing worthy of note has yet been accomplished, and never may be, though we are resolved to do our best in the directions whither our several tastes lead. We cannot fail to enlarge our ideas, at least upon the subject of Art under the guidance of and encouragement so heartily tendered by Miss May Alcott, to whose untiring energy and disinterested-ness we are indebted for all; the origin of the plan, the use of the Studio itself, and everything it contains. You will be pleased to know that among the art-books placed there by Miss Alcott, Mr. Hunt's book of 'Talks on Art', lies uppermost and claims especial notice."

Thus began Concord's first Art Center. And if to-day art flourishes within the borders of the "classic" town, as well as literature, much credit should be given to May Alcott, whose dream is coming true.

In March, 1876, the sisters returned to Concord, where they found the town all agog with its Centennial preparations. As spring advanced, the illness of Mrs. Alcott caused the daughters much anxiety, but during the summer she improved in health, and in September it was decided that May should go abroad once more, to complete the work she had relinquished when family needs had called her back from London. Of this decision Louisa wrote, "She cannot find the help she needs here, and is happy and busy in her own world over there. God be with her. She has done her distasteful duty faithfully and deserves a reward."

So it was that the elder sister again furnished May her "reward", something that none deemed needful for Louisa. Her reward, after all, was that which came from the delight of giving. For her, the *line of duty* was the only line she visualized, and she followed it ungrudgingly.

For May, the *line of beauty* ever beckoned, and she must tread its graceful curves; so they all felt, so May believed. She hesitated to leave her mother, whose failing health made them all fear that she might not be with them long. May was her baby, and her heart's delight, yet she urged her to go. If she delayed to pick up the broken threads in her art studies, it might be too late to accomplish all that she hoped for, all that they felt she must achieve. Yes, she must go.

And May wept, refused, and reconsidered, vowed she would not desert her feeble mother, and then at last reluctantly departed, holding to the belief that Marmee would still be with them for many years to come, and that since this was truly her golden opportunity, she should embrace it, for she must make the most of every chance to win success in the field she had chosen.

And so, upon September 9, 1876, she sailed back to the Old World, which held for her all that her nature craved, outside of her immediate family, and where she was destined to end a life which, if early cut off, was crowded with happiness, and from first to last crowned with fulfilled desires.

CHAPTER VI

Marmee and May

POSSIBLY the most touching of all the memorabilia of the Alcott family is a slim copy book, with marbled-paper cover and half its leaves still uninscribed, which bears upon its opening page the words: "*Mrs. Alcott's Last Diary, 1876–7.*"

Below these words is pasted a post-card picture of the Cunard steamship *China*, upon which Marmee had written, "May sails September 9, 1876."

Just ten days later, the author of "Little Women" had written on the flyleaf of this journal, "Abby May Alcott, September 19, 1876, from Louisa." And then follows Marmee's last contribution to the family records. Beginning upon the day of May's arrival at Queenstown, this journal ends upon the writer's seventy-seventh birthday, upon which date she ceased forever to wield the pen that still remains between the pages of this little book, that opens with the words:

"I dedicate this Journal to 'May', and this first page, to the joyful record of her arrival at Queenstown. The *China* (Captain Gill) made the passage in 10 days, having left at noon on the 9th, and reaching Queenstown on the 18th; on the 19th, received this note from the Cunard Steamship." (Then follows the announcement which had been sent her from the company carefully pasted into this book, with the words: "I am grateful for this prompt dispatch from this authority.")

Just ten days later, May's first letter, mailed back at Queenstown, is noted:

"Let me gratefully acknowledge the relief I enjoy on the receipt of this good news. The sad fate of Bessie Greene and Dr. Dimock fills me with apprehension lest the wild winds and many tempestuous waves may deprive me of these precious girls when on their goings and comings from foreign lands. My nerves are terribly morbid, but reason comes to my aid, and religion adjusts the balance of my faith in the unseen and eternal, and for a while I am patient, and wait, with an almost superhuman courage for the event.

"I hope to pass the next year in some profitable employment as the days occur and then by reading clever books, seeing cheerful persons, reading some, doing some light housework as my infirmities will permit of, I shall be happy and useful. Then May will be sending me nice letters and sketches, to add joy to my life, and give color to the cheerless hours of winter and indisposition."

On September 22, the writer touches upon the Art Center, which May had founded in Concord, and also upon the two young sculptors then closely associated with the Alcott family, as well as with the art interests of the town:

"Young Elwell calls to get the plaster for the head he is trying to cast. Also Dan. French calls to make kind inquiries about the arrival of his early patroness 'Miss May.' He speaks well of Elwell's talent, said he was about going to assist him in 'modelling this head' as much depended upon his beginning right in every detail. Just friendly as it should be to the young aspirant. Thinks the young people wish to carry on the 'Studio' this winter. I hope they will, as May made great exertions to initiate this Art Center in Concord. Borrowed casts from the School of Technology; and loaned her own sketches, her Portfolios and all other accessions to their benefit; Books of value for them to use with discretion, 'Hammerton on Etching', 'Ruskin on Linear Drawing', etc. I feel proud of my daughter's capability in giving this town so decided an artistic impetus. Noble girl."

MARMEE AND MAY

Extracts from May's first letter, mailed at Queenstown, follow:

My DEAR MARMEE, — While the Captain promises to keep the boat steady I scribble a line to assure you of our safe arrival; although the telegraph has long since reached you through the *Transcript*. The first two days I was pretty miserable, wondering how I could ever have left my own sweet home, lying in the close, horrid smelling berth, no air, no light; and worst of all no Marmee to pet me. The Captain came often to see me, and Dr. Hopner kindly sent me delicious pears to cool my parched mouth. By Wednesday I was feeling better and went on deck escorted by the Captain, who has been very attentive. Everybody received me with marked attention, so you see the horrors of sea life were greatly mitigated by meeting much kindness from comparative strangers.

My plan now is to go from Liverpool to Chester, thence to Warwick, on to London. The Captain offers to take my parcel back to America next week for me, so I shall try to get the hose for you and Louisa. The Scotch Lady, one passenger in the *China*, spoke charmingly of Louisa as a writer, and begged to see her picture if I had one, which of course I had. She talked much of her, and her work, "Little Women," ever so much; Dr. Hopner and Captain Gill all sung praises. The lady begged me to visit her if I came to Scotland. Louisa's fame reaches over the seas and makes a welcome for us everywhere. I hope to get off a long letter for you next week; kiss all around, not forgetting Rosa. I dream of the Star on her forehead. [Rosa was May's saddle horse.]

"I have thus transcribed the parts of dear May's letter," writes her mother, "because it seems always more precious than anything which may come after, as it is the assurance from her hand that she is there bodily safe. Let me be thankful to God for this and all other mercies. I seem to be living beyond the length of days allotted to most, and yet my blessings are without number still."

Proofs of her sister's popularity in England greeted May on arrival and she wrote of an incident which occurred in a railway carriage soon after she left Liverpool:

"We stopped at a small station and a charming young girl got in. Looking up I was much pleased to find myself opposite a fresh-faced English girl in a seal-skin jacket and jaunty hat. And now, oh

distinguished sister, comes the gist of this my first
adventure. As I sat apparently absorbed in my
accounts, endeavoring to get a clear notion of
£. s. d., I was a little surprised to have my neighbor begin the conversation, for if history is to be
believed the English as a nation are not given to
much conversation with strangers. Seeing she was
intent on being sociable I, of course, was but too
happy to continue the conversation and from talking of the speed at which our mail-train was bearing us along, we got to comparing English and
American ways, then pictures, artists, writers, and
speaking of Dickens and how widely his books
were read everywhere, my companion said:

"'Ah but you are not any more familiar with
English novels than we with your American ones,
and just now our great delight is in a Miss Alcott,
who writes the most charming books I have ever
read. I have such a desire to take her by the
hand and tell her how infinitely I admire "Jo", in
"Little Women", and how eagerly we look for
everything from her pen.'

"Well, you can imagine I was a little surprised to
hear this fine English girl speak of you so familiarly
and in terms of such honest praise. The fun of
the thing struck me instantly, as she could in no

way imagine who I was, as the M. A. on my travelling-bag told no tales; it might mean Mary Ann, Miserable Artist, or a thousand other things. So I said quite coolly, though I could n't keep down a flush of real delight at this most un-expected compliment to my best of sisters, 'What do you find to like in them? I should imagine they were far too American in their style to entirely please you, for though the boys and girls talk and act like them at home, yet some of their perform-ances must rather astonish you.'

" 'Well perhaps it's because we have known so many Americans, and make allowance for the greater freedom in so many ways, allowed particu-larly to your young girls, that these stories seem so natural and real. And not only that, but they are so thoroughly good, always having a moral very sweetly put to the reader. In short, Papa was so carried away by them that at Christmas he bought many copies to give away as the most profitable and enjoyable present he could find.'

"Upon this I said, 'It certainly pleases me exceedingly to hear you speak so enthusiastically about Miss Alcott, as she is my sister, and I shall have the pleasure of telling her her name has become a household word in one English family at least. I am only sorry I have not a photograph of her to give you since you admire "Jo" so much and she is said to resemble her.'

"For a minute my companion looked perfectly amazed and incredulous then smiled, blushed and seemed so uncomfortable that I partly from consideration for her, and partly from real hunger (having had such an early breakfast) took out my lunch of sandwiches, made up at the hotel for me, and some preserved ginger left from the generous supply put into my bag at East Boston, and chatting and eating she forgot her embarrassment, . . . after a little hesitation she led the conversation back again to her favorite theme Miss Alcott, saying there was one thing that seemed a little overdrawn and that was in 'Little Men', the Professor making the boy whip him instead of his punishing the boy.

" 'Well' I said, 'I don't wonder at your thinking so, but it really happened,' and I then gave her a little sketch of father's ideas of a school, and described his experiences in the Masonic Temple as far as I could. She seemed very much interested and asked about Lu's hospital life, all of which I was delighted to tell her, and rattled on about our family till I was ashamed to say another word, and was glad when we reached her station, for leaving me, which she did in a truly unEnglish hearty way that surprised me. Coming and taking my hand she said, 'I have to thank you for a most delightful journey, and I dare not tell you how grateful I am for the good fortune that has thrown us together,' and smiling and bowing she disappeared with the guard, leaving me much amused at the whole affair and very much wishing we might meet again, but as no addresses were exchanged between us, I fear there is little hope of it in this endlessly big city. Here ends my first adventure though not my last."

Upon October 22, Mrs. Alcott notes the receipt of a letter from Chester, some of which she transcribes, but which may be inserted here more fully:

"Here I sit in a cozy little parlor of 'The Blossoms' after sightseeing round this quaint place all day. . . . I took my sketch-book and sauntered forth into the warm sunshine about the happiest woman on the globe. Then I went to the old wall which entirely surrounds the most ancient part of the town, though there are more houses now outside than inside of it. From this narrow walk which I followed entirely round, I got a fine view of everything, coming first to the old red sandstone pile called *The Phoenix Tower*, from which

Charles I watched the fatal battle on Marston Moor, the old Roman wall being built 61 A.D.

"Then on to the great water-tower which makes one corner of the wall, and which, half covered with ivy, was quite too lovely to pass, but I felt there was still something better at St. John's Church for me. And tho' the church itself had been a great deal restored, the fine Norman architecture was very impressive, and when the rosy-faced sexton, whom I had sought out, opened a wide iron gate into the graveyard, where stood a beautiful group of red stone arches, hung with ivy, and pretty glimpses of distant hills and water above, the very green grass at their base, I thought it about the most beautiful bit I had ever seen. The colors came quickly out, and slipping a shilling into my guide's hand, I told him to leave me for an hour or two, and I got something to take the place of the old Kenilworth bit you all liked.

"Then to the wall again which I had not finished and on to the Cathedral, which is considered so fine. Certainly the soft gilded frescoes of the roof have the richest effect possible, being to my eye in better taste and more effective than anything we saw in the French cathedrals, or even St. Marks at Venice. The figures were like the Fra Angelico angels on a large scale, with the great lines of division held together by antique knots of fine gilded fret-work, the organ being held high up above the congregation by three massive pillars curving from a narrow base upward like a lily. The cloisters were damp and mouldy enough to suit me, and I enjoyed the whole expedition immensely, bringing up in a bun-shop opposite the entrance where I ate a Banbury cake and drank a glass of milk with a relish. Then home by some curiosity-shops, where the old chests and chairs nearly drove me wild, for they were such impossible articles to carry along with me that I could only howl over them and pass by. Such beauties for ten shillings that would be fifty dollars in *Doll's* sanctum, that with my love of good bargains it was maddening. The most beautiful ones here right under the old Bishop's house, the front of which I send you in the photograph. The side-walks are mostly arcade fashion, the houses and shops reaching over and making pretty lines of arches, through which the figures come toward one like actors on a stage. I wish Lu were here to breathe the soft air and enjoy the peculiar beauty of England which can never be described. Now my disagreeable voyage is over and I begin to enjoy things and every day will be a new delight which I shall faithfully relate to you."

MARMEE AND MAY

Mrs. Alcott next writes of May's stay at Stratford, and of her arrival in London:

"Miss Pratt arrives today and brings letters from May who met her at the lodgings in Osborne Place. She brings me a pair of large hose and a sweet picture from Stratford-on-Avon, also a flower from the foot of the old arches at St. John's Church, Chester; everything seems propitious."

On the reverse side of this page of the journal Mrs. Alcott has inserted a little photograph of Shakespeare's birthplace, and beneath it a bit of ivy.

May's letter follows:

Stratford, Sept. 21, 1876.

DEAR MARMEE: — I send an ivy leaf and little flower which I picked for your journal, from the foot of the old arches at St. John's Church, Chester. I had not intended to write again until arriving in London, but the temptation to fill the time while waiting for my poached eggs and beer is too strong, as I can no longer sight-see, it being after seven P.M., and I have no one to talk to and tell my adventures to but you.

I left Chester this morning at 9 o'clock after a

farewell look at the very dear old furniture rich with carving, and I reached here at 2 o'clock, grasped my colors and went forth immediately, and did Anne Hathaway's cottage after eating a bun at Mrs. Plunket's, for it is so much cheaper to eat a good luncheon at a shop than order things at the hotels. This is the "Shakespeare Inn", which I chose in preference to the "Red Horse", tho' I wonder I did n't take the latter if only for love of Rosa. At Chester, the "Bear's Paw" was just opposite my window, which name I thought most amusing. I shall give until noon to doing the Shakespeare house; the room in which he was born I send enclosed to please Mother, then at 12 take the train for London. . . .

I had a fright in my dreams at Chester last night about mother and do hope nothing has happened to make her sick since I left. Nan must tell me all the household items. . . . It's a very dear old place and I should like to spend the rest of my days here tho' everyone seems poor, for most of the people seem to trade on the reputation of the great man, and beyond that there is not much doing I should imagine. Over every door in this hotel is the name of one of his plays and over mine is "Romeo and Juliet", which I hope means that there is to be a little romance in my life.

The next entry is penned by Mrs. Alcott on her seventy-sixth birthday, the last but one that she was destined to celebrate; she notes that her grandsons are recovering from typhoid fever:

"8th Oct. Glorious bright day, the air is full of color, my mercies thicken fast; good news from dear May, Johnny rapidly recovering, Freddy well, Anna and Louisa still saved from infection of typhoid; although they have been over the patient little fellow for eight days. But my blessings are renewed every day and I am here to receive and record the same.

> Thus far the Lord has led me on,
> Thus far his power prolongs my days!
> And every evening shall make known
> Some fresh memorial of his Grace!

"This afternoon the remains of our friend Miss Sophia Thoreau are brought here (her former home) for interring. The family close with her. Henry her brother died in 1864, the mother in '72. Their Cemetery Lot is near ours, which contains only the dear dust of my Lizzie, and close by the bones of our Beloved John Pratt.

"My birthday was celebrated tenderly by gifts, fruit, flowers, frills. From Johnny note-paper of various tints, very handsome."

[137]

At this point two youthful inscriptions that had accompanied her grandson's gifts were pasted into the journal: the first said — "Grandma from Johnny", with the words no doubt supplied by an older hand:

> Hid in this box
> Pretty paper doth dwell;
> A loving wish
> And a very good smell.

While the gift from Freddy was supplemented with the suggestion:

> A tidy tie
> For grandma's neck,
> When the new ruffs
> Her bosom deck.

And the recipient pens the words, "From Freddy, 'barbe' very useful, pretty black lace frille."

After a stay in London, May travels on to Paris, which is her goal, and there she joins her friends, the Misses Peckham, in comfortable lodgings, and is soon working diligently under the instruction of Monsieur Krug, in his well-lighted studio, at 11 Boulevard Clichy, of which she writes:

"It is devoted to female students in all branches of art, and where the much discussed question of the propriety of women's studying from the nude is settled in a delicate and proper manner by the gentlemanly director. Here one has the great advantage of severe and discriminating criticism, two mornings each week, from Monsieur Carl Müller, the painter of the well-known 'Conciergerie during the Reign of Terror', hanging in the Luxembourg, and the recipient of every honor France has to bestow on a man of genius. Monsieur Cot, and the sculptor, Carrière Belleuse, also visit the class to inspect the afternoon and evening drawings. Monsieur Krug's prices are moderate, being one hundred francs per month, for two daily and one evening séance, with no extra charge for the excellent models provided, or for towels, soap etc."

May suggests that this is on some accounts the best place for American girls to study in Paris, since many of the ateliers are overcrowded, badly managed, or afford objectionable companionship; she goes on to say, however, that "pupils or admirers of each leading painter sing his especial praises loud and long, and among those who receive ladies are —Monsieurs Chaplin, Duran, Cabanel, Jackson, Luminais, Bouguereau, Robert Fleury, and Lefebre."

"Then [she continues] there is Julien's upper and lower school, in Passage Panorama, where a student receives criticism from the first leading authorities, and is surrounded by splendidly strong work on the easels of the many faithful French, who for years have crowded the dirty, close rooms, though I believe the lower school as it is called, or male class, no longer opens its doors to women, for the price being but one half of the upper school, attracted too many. Also, with better models, and a higher standard of work, it was found impossible that women should paint from the living nude models of both sexes, side by side with the Frenchmen.

"This is a sad conclusion to arrive at, when one remembers the brave efforts made by a band of American ladies some years ago, who supported one another with such dignity and modesty, in a steadfast purpose under this ordeal, that even Parisians, to whom such a type of womanly character was unknown and almost incomprehensible, were forced into respect and admiration of the simple earnestness and purity which proved a sufficient protection from even their evil tongues; M. Julien himself confessing that if all ladies exercised the beneficial influence of a certain Madonna-faced Miss N. among them, anything would be possible.

"Something besides courage was needed for such a triumph; and women of no other nationality could have accomplished it; though it must be acknowledged, a like clique will not easily be met with again. So, let those who commonly represent the indiscreet, husband-hunting butterfly, as the typical American girl abroad, at least do her the justice to put this fact on record, to her credit."

Conscious of Marmee's intense interest in every detail of her life in Paris, May describes most minutely the little ménage which she shares with her friends the Misses Peckham:

DEAR MARMEE, — Since there are no events of startling interest to relate to you week by week, I will proceed to tell you just how I spend each day at present in this gay city. Firstly, we are having and have had for two weeks or more the most splendid, warm, bright weather, most inviting to go about, tho' we do not improve it in that way. For I rise at seven o'clock, partly dress myself and slip on L's old flannel gown and in my blue scufflers I take ten steps from my cozy little room to the kitchen and put a match to a dozen bits of charcoal which is quite sufficient to warm a pail of chocolate for our first meal. This, in a generous bowl with one of the little loaves, or rolls, such as only France can produce, lasts me during the morning. At eight, a short walk of five or ten minutes brings me to Monsieur Krug's studio . . . and here I find a living model posing with

only a band round the waist, and work at a drawing of him, or her (as it may happen) till twelve.
Then run home to a nice hot breakfast, and back
again at one, to paint till five o'clock, or dark,
whenever that chooses to descend upon us busy
mortals, and put an end to our work.

We dine at six o'clock, and the evening finds me
too tired to do much more than write a French
exercise or make my bed and get into it. So you
see the reason you don't get more letters from your
baby, and why they can tell you so little when
you get them. . . . This week, we have a perfectly superb model, an Italian of fine rich color,
grand physique and the head of a god, with great
soft eyes, proud dilating nostrils, and dark mous-
tache, while his black hair curls all over his finely
shaped head. Would n't you call him a beauty?
Particularly if you could see him with his head
tossed back, eyes raised; he stands like a statue
for an hour without moving a muscle; you can't
wonder we admire the beautiful creature. . . . He
has been a model for years and is so proud of his
perfect posing that his indignation knew no bounds,
when one of the ladies suggested he was n't quite
in the position, and with a scornful look he threw
himself into it and would take no further notice
of any remarks we made. There are fourteen pupils

THE SALON AT *RUE MANSART*, 1877
From a pen sketch by May Alcott

in the morning, all Americans, or English, but one Frenchwoman, and in the P.M. almost as many only a younger set of ladies. Mon. Krug is a nice gentlemanly man, and a good teacher; then we have three of the best painters in France who come and criticize twice a week. If I could find time I would write a letter about it to the *Transcript*, for it's been so hard for ladies to find the best advantages here without paying exorbitantly for the same, that we want our sister artists to know of it.

About this time May writes of a drive through the woods, which makes her long for a ride with her mother, and her own horse, through the Concord lanes:

"We have just had a lovely ride in the Bois, and as it was race day and all the world abroad, we enjoyed it heaps, for the wood itself is lovely being so deep and shady, and as full of ferns, Solomon's seal, and field flowers as any of our woods at home. I imagined Marmee beside me, while I drove Rosa, and forgetting all the dress parade, paint and fashion, saw myself in the pretty Lincoln roads with the nice fresh smell so like the taste of wild strawberries. It is so charming to see the children and crowds of grown people either in the boats on the lakes, or in the many rustic towers or arbors all about, rambling round as if there was nothing else to do in the world either for young or old. Elegant private carriages stood about, while the lofty couples with their children walked or picked flowers up and down the shady avenues or wood-paths, for they are not a bit like those in common parks but kept wild and beautiful with grand driveways for those of more haughty taste. The 'demis', as we call the gay women of the demi-monde, were out driving themselves, dressed in green velvet suits, or their evening dresses, fine to see, with servants in livery, but their blackened eyes, painted cheeks and lips told who they were."

Towards the close of November, a long and cheerful letter from Mrs. Alcott brings forth an enthusiastic reply:

MY DEAR MARMEE, — Your long beaming letter welcomed me when I returned hungry and in haste at noon today from school, and before touching the nice little *déjeuner à la fourchette*, which Kate had invitingly spread ready for us, I read aloud your letter which was interesting all round, though the household items had a particular interest for me, which they could have to no one who did not know the crooks and turns of our family.

As soon as I land on this side it always seems as

if I were someone else, whose actions I followed with interest but took no actual part in, and in a measure I lose my identity and feel like a heroine in some novel more than anything else. At present there is nothing in the least like a romance going on, but still it is quite different from Concord and its surroundings. As I told mother in my last letter my days are much alike, drawing and painting from eight o'clock A.M. until dark, and to bed early, unless callers come as they sometimes do.

Leland, from Boston, last night made us a long visit, talking hard all the time. He is young and handsome and will make his mark in our big city when he returns in the Spring as he intends doing. . . . Lippincott from Philadelphia dropped in, and Moss also, who is the intimate friend of Mrs. Owen Wister, to whom I have promised a letter of introduction to Alice Bartlett, for he goes to Rome for a few months and she will like him, not only as Mrs. Wister's most intimate friend and cousin, but also because he is a good painter and interesting man, having lived here for years and been in society a good deal and is a brilliant talker. Madam d'Alembert, to whose reception I told you we went, is a countess, this Moss being her nephew . . .

The Peckhams and I went to see a great picture that Mr. Moss is painting, hoping it will be accepted for the Salon, which is the great exhibition in May. He told us he would have what he called "Lady Day", as his picture is an "Eve", and he thought some would prefer to see it when he was not present, so he set a day for them especially, but I said "No, we prefer to come and criticize it to your face rather than behind your back, and what we shall see on the walls of the exhibition we can very properly look at in your studio." This pleased him and we had a fine time seated in great carved papal chairs, or gilded ones of Louis XIV time, before an immense picture elegantly framed, with fine tapestries for hangings, and sconces, brass church lamps, carved cabinets and imperial mirrors strewn in great profusion everywhere. I frankly said I did not like an affectation of modesty in a nude figure, and that the long golden hair blown across the front in place of a fig-leaf looked very forced and unnatural. They all agreed with me, but otherwise it was thought fine and it will do him great credit, for it is thought the most difficult matter in Art to succeed in a perfect nude, so all the artists great and small attempt it for practice, and the shops are full of them. Some bring most splendid bits of flesh, soft and creamy. You see everything is Art and artists here so I have nothing to write about but these.

Some of the young men who went to Rome for the winter are coming back scared by the fever there, so I am glad I am not in Italy, for this climate seems to suit me excellently, it being just cold enough to wear thick things and to light fires, yet so far it is bright and clear. . . . Think of me among good friends, with two Concordians just around the corner, plenty to do, and enough to live on. What more could one desire? Tonight, I am in my red silk dress, writing at our big round table, with a student-lamp, lots of books, pictures, pretty hangings and furniture, and Kate with her lovely auburn hair in a grand pile on the top of her head, and her pretty delicate profile in strong relief, to refresh my eyes whenever I look up, to blunder out some French phrase to her, for we make good resolutions to talk the foreign tongue all we possibly can.

About this time she writes describing their housekeeping:

"All is so simple when there are no servants and all our five rooms are so near each other, and the kitchen so small and convenient that one accomplishes the work easily enough and it's like keeping house in a doll's mansion, no running up and down stairs, for things to tire one, but only a step from one room to another, and no thick carpets to sweep and hold the dust, but clean polished floors. This kind of housekeeping I don't object to, for it leaves the daylight for painting and the twilight hours are well passed in washing dishes and general clearing up for the evening and next day."

A fortnight later she describes their celebration of Thanksgiving:

"We had a turkey of noble proportions, costing eleven francs, which was a little extravagant considering our usually simple ménage, but has proved a *pièce de resistance*, as Channing would say. For Kate (whose talents lie in the culinary direction) stuffed it in a most savory manner and with celery, vegetables and gravy, baked pears, cake and sweet pudding, nuts, raisins and coffee made a fine repast, which was eagerly devoured by three jolly spinsters after various confabs and rather tumultuous conclaves held in the kitchen, where the quarters are so limited that one had to repose on the range, the other on the potato-box, while the third moved cautiously round the small space allowed for action. Rose tossed up some little meat *pâtés*, such as they had eaten in Holland,

Mays room in 11 rue Mansart.
Paris.

MAY'S PARIS BEDROOM, 1877
From a pen sketch by May Alcott

and at intervals while she basted the noble bird in our oven, almost too small to hold his swelling breast, Kate and I played dominoes on a board held between our knees. I have learned the game lately as it is much more a test of one's wits than the mere matching numbers, as I will show you when I come, for it does n't try your eyes like cards and I can enjoy it better than chess.

"Tonight after school, in velvet, silk and my new bonnet and tossing yellow flower, I went with Kate to call on Madame Bigot, née Healy, as she left her card with 'Wednesday' on it to inform me of her reception day. We found only three of the daughters present and Pa Healy and a French lady jabbering away with Madame B. She was very pleasant and I thanked her for the books to you. I told her Marston had orders to send yours to her. In your preface, I should have liked it better if you had said *to the roses preparing to bloom*, instead of *getting ready to bloom*, which is a little awkward. . . . This afternoon they gave us a cup of tea and talked Paris and Art, and the party came out quite determined to go tomorrow evening to the Healy's first reception, and see what it is like. At school today they told me the H's gave the finest balls and parties in Paris, so I will report all about it."

May closes with the words, penned a day later, "After all we did n't go to the party for I came home so tired."

G. P. A. Healy, whose portraits enjoyed a wide popularity for many years, will probably be best remembered for certain historical compositions; among them "Franklin Urging the Cause of the Colonies before Louis XVI" is widely known, as well as "Webster Replying to Hayne in the Senate", which to-day hangs in Faneuil Hall, Boston.

In her home letters, May frequently refers to her friend Mary Cassatt, whose work she greatly admired, and whose friendship she highly prized. Miss Cassatt, who was five years her senior, was a Philadelphian, but her father's family were of French extraction, and she had spent her early years in Paris, returning with her parents to spend a decade in Philadelphia, and then in 1868 beginning her art career in Europe. After some years spent in the studios of various masters, Mary Cassatt had settled in Paris to make her permanent home there, so that both by inheritance and by adoption she belonged rather more to France than to America. Yet to-day she is counted among the foremost of the American painters who have won fame in the Art world.

Before her meeting with May Alcott, in 1876, she had joined the group of Impressionists that Degas had drawn about him, and though she received no formal instruction from this master, he greatly influenced her work. He welcomed her pictures in the exhibitions of this new school, which was then frowned upon by members of the older school, whose representatives expressed their disapproval of Mary Cassatt's later work by the rejection of her pictures at the Salon of 1877, although she had been represented at several previous Salons.

Early in November, 1876, May describes a tea party at Miss Cassatt's beautiful studio, where they met various New York friends, and ate "fluffy cream and chocolate, with French cakes, while sitting in carved chairs, on Turkish rugs, with superb tapestries as a background, and fine pictures on the walls looking down from their splendid frames."

"Statues and articles of *vertu* filled the corners, the whole being lighted by a great antique hanging lamp. We sipped our *chocolat* from superior china, served on an India waiter, upon an embroidered cloth of heavy material. Miss Cassatt was charming as usual in two shades of brown satin and rep, being very lively and a woman of real genius, she will be a first-class light as soon as her pictures get a little circulated and known, for they are handled in a masterly way, with a touch of strength one seldom finds coming from a woman's fingers. They would n't suffer if hung with the Thomas Lawrences."

She describes another social affair where many Philadelphians gathered:

"Sunday night the Ramseys opened the winter festivities by having a reception, and we went and met stacks of artists, there being but few ladies, and row upon row of young and old masculines, all painters and interesting accordingly; again, we sat upon antique couches, in strange chairs amid Japanese works of all kinds, and superb velvet and tapestried cushions and heard some lovely songs by a Mr. Bush, in a fine tenor voice. He escorted us home and promised to come and give me a regular funeral of all the dirges he knew. We had grapes, wine of the best, cake, and the gentlemen cigarettes after we had left the room. Mrs. Ramsey is a cozy little woman, who with her artistic husband entertains all the young Americans who are staying here, particularly those from Philadelphia, as the R's hail from there. They all talked pictures and art generally and I had a lovely evening feeling as much at home as possible, talking over Boston and its lights with Blashfield and Pierce. Three of them live together with a *bonne* to cook for them, and are to have a house-warming soon, as all are just returning from the summer trips. They are a hard-working set, painting like beavers from models all day, and some of them all the evening too, at the schools, as gas-light is thought excellent for studying shadows. I talked with as many as fifteen of these students on this evening, some of them already known for their good work. All Paris, and artists, and no other profession seems so fashionable, tho' this is no place to sell any but great pictures, many being painted for the American and English market."

A letter written on December 12th refers to various Americans then in Paris, and to the news that they bring of mutual friends:

"I had hardly dressed myself for the evening when in came Mr. Bradford and Mr. Sedgwick, both very jolly and cordial. The former tells me that Una Hawthorne is engaged to an American whom she met at Julien's, who lives at Twickenham. So now I am more than ever left behind in the race for matrimony. Also, he said Rose had a child and was very happy about it, as was Una at her engagement."

The romance in Una Hawthorne's life, to which May refers, was destined to be only too brief, ending in deepest sadness with the sudden death of the man she hoped to marry. After her mother's passing in London, in the winter of 1871, Una remained in England for some years, devoting herself to the care of destitute children; then she lived for a time with her brother in Dresden, returning to New York to visit her sister Rose, who had married George Parsons Lathrop. While there, she became well acquainted with Albert Webster, a gifted young writer, whose work was deemed unusually promising, and who, on her return to England to rejoin her brother, wrote asking her hand in marriage. Una accepted him, and a bright future seemed opening before them, but Webster's health was very delicate, and a trip to the Sandwich Islands was recommended; he started on this journey in search of health but became desperately ill and died upon the voyage.

The tragic news was sent to Una by a friend, who wrote her the sad tidings, and as she read the letter, she seemed calm and unmoved, giving way to no passionate grief or terrible emotion, but from that moment she was completely changed, seeming like one who had relinquished earthly things and who dwelt in the spiritual world. She made no change in her accustomed occupations, but in a year her lovely auburn hair had become gray and she seemed to have grown prematurely old. In the summer of 1877, she died at Clewer, near Windsor, where she had been spending the summer at a small Protestant convent, and serving meanwhile as district visitor. She was buried at Kensal Green, beside her beloved mother, whom she had nursed through her last illness in London, six years before, and who in early days had nursed her so untiringly during those cruel months when her life hung upon a thread from Roman fever. She was the eldest of the Hawthorne children, and seems to have been the most richly endowed, with graces both of mind and body, — a child in every way worthy of her two parents. She had a brilliant intellect and a lovely unselfish nature, but after her long months of illness in Rome she was never so robust as formerly, and with the added sorrows which came to her she seemed like a beautiful bit of porcelain shattered by the rude hand of a relentless fate.

Another of May's communications touches upon the meeting with a family friend and poet, whose charming verse and wide acquaintance with her fellow writers on both sides of the water won for her international recognition, both as a writer and as a hostess, — Louise Chandler Moulton.

At about this period, a publication entitled "Famous Women" was in the process of compilation, and Mrs. Moulton had been asked to contribute a biographical sketch of Louisa Alcott, a suggestion not welcomed by the subject save in rare instances; yet in response to this request, the latter wrote to this personal friend:

"I have not the least objection to your writing a sketch of L. M. A. I shall feel quite comfortable in your hands. I have little material to give you; but in 'Little Women' you will find the various stages of my career and experience. Don't forget to mention that I don't like lion-hunters, and that I don't serve autophotos and biographies to the hundreds of boys and girls who ask, and that I heartily endorse Dr. Holmes's views on this subject."

May wrote in reference to this Boston friend who was then leaving Paris to spend the Christmas season in England, "To-night we go to see Mrs. Moulton, who starts for a visit to London this week to stay with a Miss Marston, her intimate friend there, for the holidays."

This reference to Miss Marston recalls the fact
that it was at about this time that Mrs. Moulton's
association began with the blind poet, Philip
Bourke Marston, whose friend and biographer she
became and with whose sister she often stayed in
England.

In recalling her first meeting with the blind poet
Mrs. Moulton wrote:

"It was just six weeks before his twenty-sixth
birthday. He was tall, slight, and in spite of his
blindness, graceful. He had a noble and beautiful
forehead. His brown eyes were perfect in shape,
and even in color, save for a dimness like a white
mist that obscured the pupil, but which you per-
ceived only when you were quite near to him. . . .
His face was singularly refined, but his lips were
full and pleasure-loving, and suggested dumbly
how cruel must be the limitations of blindness to a
nature hungry for love and for beauty. I had been
greatly interested, before seeing him, in his poems,
and to meet him was a memorable delight. . . .
He and his sister, who was his inseparable companion, soon became my close friends, and with
them both this friendship lasted till the end."

In February, 1887, ten years after this first
meeting, Philip Bourke Marston died. He be-

queathed to Mrs. Moulton his books and manuscripts as well as many autographs of great value,
and he also requested that she become his literary
executor, a labor of love which she performed to
the best of her ability, writing some years later:

"I was named by Mr. Marston, in his will, as
his literary executor. I brought out after his death
a volume whose contents he had not heretofore
included in any book, and which I called 'A Last
Harvest.' Then I put all his flower-poems together
(as he had long wished to do) in a volume entitled
'Garden Secrets.' Finally, I have brought out a
collected edition of his poems, including three
volumes published before his death, and the ones
I had compiled after he died."

Thus did Mrs. Moulton conclude her gift of
loving service to one whose friendship she had
prized so dearly. Of this poet's life, lived in total
darkness, she said:

"You may well call his life tragic. He was only
three years old when he lost his sight. He was
educated orally, but his knowledge of literature
was a marvel. The poets of the past were his
familiar friends and he could repeat Swinburne's
poems by the hour. . . . Some of the best critics

in London declared that the author of 'Song Tide' (Marston's first volume) should by virtue of this one book, take equal rank with Swinburne, Morris and Rossetti . . . and I feel that when Philip Bourke Marston died, at the age of thirty-seven, England lost one of her noblest and subtlest poets."

Whether or not May Alcott came in touch with the gifted, blind poet it is not possible to state, but it is certain that she and Mrs. Moulton were both in London in 1877, where they doubtless enjoyed much the same circle of literary and artistic friends, even as they did in Paris.

Marmee's journal, which had been laid aside for several weeks, again bore traces of her pen, and she wrote on Christmas day:

"We celebrate by interchange of gifts, give and receive. The boys have their stockings crammed with goodies, and Anna and Louisa furnish a table of pretty things for old and young; a work-basket with the following verses for me:

WITH A WORK BASKET FOR MARMEE

For the busy hands, that seldom rest,
A neat new basket, I have dresst
Mittens all holes, and broken breeches,
There will come for tidy stitches;
Brand new shirts, and ragged gloves,
To make and mend, Grandma loves;

MAY ALCOTT

And as she sits in her big Chair,
May gentle time, herself repair.
                        LOUISA M. ALCOTT, Dec. 25, 1876."

Concerning these gifts the recipient writes:

"Each present was accompanied with appropriate lines, which I have always valued more than the articles, because more enduring as 'love offerings', warm from the heart of the giver, like Prayer, 'The motion of a hidden fire, that trembles in the breast'."

The final entry in this journal for 1876 recalls the wide interest which had been awakened throughout the country by the Exposition at Philadelphia, and also the closely contested presidential election.

"Dec. 31, 1876. The last day of this Centennial year commemorated by the great world's 'Exposition', at Philadelphia. On account of the prolonged contest for the presidential vote owing to false counts at the South, and questionable returns made by the clerks as well as Electors, the Senate will finally have to decide on one of the candidates, or choose a new one, among so many factions, and choice now will probably lead to great dissatisfaction among the Republicans and Democrats; as a family we have had a comfortable year. Louisa has published 'Silver Pitchers', and 'Rose in Bloom', this year, besides several stories; her popularity increases. May's absence is much mitigated by her pleasant letters, and pictures she sends me, and wholly compensated for in the fact of her advantages of Society and Art Culture she enjoys in Paris. I close the brief record of the year 1876 with great gratitude for the comforts I enjoy."

CHAPTER VII

Marmee's Journal

THE opening of the New Year, the last she was destined to see on earth, is cheerfully recorded by Mrs. Alcott, on January 1, 1877:

"We are all in good health and spirits. Brilliant, beautiful day. The year comes in festively; its gorgeous drapery of clouds of many colors. Not cold. I sew a little for Louisa. Freddy played the piano last night, the last tune, 'America.' Ushers in the New Year with his favorite waltz (*Star*). We take a sleigh-ride, call at Mrs. Pratt's. I still find much difficulty in getting into a carriage; otherwise I am very well, and enjoy life in a tranquil partial serenity I hardly thought I could reach after such a disturbed condition of the nervous system."

The entries from the journal which follow are interspersed with quotations from May's letters, reflecting from day to day the art life of the youngest daughter and her activities in Paris, of which she writes early in January:

"You will like to hear of our pleasant little episode at the studios which seems to be the only thing of interest to relate as happening this week. Monsieur Müller, who comes to correct our drawings, has been faithfully twice a week, ever since the beginning of the school, late in September, and as he does not receive any pay for his services, I suggested that as we were under obligation to him for his kindness, it would be a pretty compliment to send him a fine bouquet on New Year's day, as that is the only gift day in France. My suggestion was immediately taken up and voted to be done without fail, the flowers not to cost more than thirty francs. Two of the ladies were deputed to order the flowers and see that all was done *comme il faut*. New Year's day came and most of the students went down as usual, and at an early hour the bouquet arrived, a great loose bunch of white lilacs, a few small rose-buds, and some other ordinary white flowers with no taste or no beauty about it.

"Then there was a general howl and we protested we would not receive it, and certainly would not offer such an ordinary thing to Monsieur Müller. Mr. Krug looked at it with surprise and giving the bearer *pour boire* sent him off saying we should n't take it. Then in consternation at our dilemma two of the English girls went off resolved to find something really beautiful, and succeeded in getting a lovely bunch of roses, camelias, ferns, and effective waving things, paying only ten francs for it. One of them bearing it in triumph to M. Müller, who, when he came to correct, paid a pretty compliment to us in the way of thanks, saying he appreciated the attention of our 'sending our *photographs* to him on New Year's day.'

"Was n't that pretty to liken us to flowers? When he came to my drawing, of a full-length negro, who is really the 'Prince of Timbuctoo', and such a splendid specimen of a man that he looks very princely, Müller said: 'With what passion and enthusiasm you draw this ensemble; it is very vigorous and shows your interest and not scorn of the race.' I could n't answer him, as this was all said in French, but it amused the class as I, among them, had pretty freely expressed my admiration for him, beside fighting the battle of the blacks versus the whites, whenever the question came up between the Southerners, of whom there are three in the class, and two of us Northerners. I am proud that he proves my part of the proposition, as most true, for he is the most gentlemanly, polite and delicate model that we have had. He was in the Crimean War and showed us four great scars on his legs where he was wounded, and Mr. Krug told us he was decorated for his courage, and considered one of the best models in Paris.

"My drawings improve from week to week, and now I can draw the human figure without great difficulty, which is quite a triumph, it being the most difficult thing possible to put on paper, and have action in it, and the individuality of each model. . . . Marmee will like to know that I have bought a pretty little graceful basket and lined it, trimmed it with light blue silk for a work-basket, and everyone admires it, it is so dressy and pretty, and Marmee's gold thimble reposes in it for looks. Though I have sewed a little lately altering Lu's velvet jacket to fit tight over the hips so that with my velvet skirt and silk overskirt it has a festive appearance.

"When I become rich and great, I shall found a school for indigent artists and aspiring young students, as Rosa Bonheur has done in Paris, for girls under twenty years of age. I have still thirty more years to work in and think of, if I am spared, that I may do something in that time. Things certainly look most promising just now and I have painted a head of 'Christ' (that is the model we have who has sat so much for Christ that he goes now by that name) which Miss Austin, who is the best painter in the studio, held it up for all to see, saying she considered 'that luminous flesh', and all asked what colors I had used, which considering I was a beginner was flattering to say the least."

The receipt of this letter is noted in the journal with an approving comment, and the words:

"Good child, we know very well, she does all things well, her capabilities are much in her eyes and fingers. As a child I observed with what ease and grace she did little things. In 1856, she made a Crayon Sketch of her mother, quite remarkable for a girl of 16 years of age, under Mr. Murdock's instructions, and that skilful hand and nice eye have been developing ever since. She copies Turner most successfully, Ruskin says."

Marmee closes with a suggestion upon which the artist daughter later comments mirthfully:

"May says, 'I think I shall adopt the style of Millet.' I rather wonder at this, for a notice of this artist in the *Harper's Monthly*, March, 1877, speaks of this style of coloring as being dry and hard."

A few days after the previous communication May writes, contrasting the Paris winter with that in Concord:

My dear Marmee, — I have only just received a nice fat letter from Lu and Nan, dated Dec. 24th and though I have mailed two this week for my Marmee, I will be extravagant enough to mail still another if it's any comfort to you, snowed up in dreary Concord. Everything is so warm and bright, the grass being so beautifully green in the Tuileries Gardens, that I can hardly imagine the cold you describe. To-day I rose early and feeling like taking a rampage to refresh my mind and stretch my legs a little after the work of the week, I started forth walking to the Louvre where Rose was to meet me, as she chose to ride by bus. But the air was so soft and springlike, the streets clean and dry sidewalks that I skipped along to rue Rivoli wondering in what part of it Louisa abode so many years ago. The gardens are superb and I like that quarter of Paris very much if it were only nearer Krug's and the studios. All the artists' clubs are together in this part and if not so aristocratic it is sociable.

In letters that follow, May describes seeing "Laddie", whose friend and benefactor Louisa had proved a decade earlier. He was at this time living in Paris with his mother, and often joined May on her shopping expeditions, aiding her in the search for bargains. Of her success in this respect she writes:

"I like no better fun of a Sunday than to meander along stopping to look in at all the shop windows, for they are most fascinating and curious, especially the bric-à-brac collections. As I went through the Palais Royal I looked at Gibbet watches, the same ones that Laddie asked the prices of for me when I first came, and found a much handsomer one than Alice's, with a pretty head, key and place for monogram, for $25 which considering it was watch and chain in one, I bought, not having any, and finding it very inconvenient sometimes to be entirely without the time. Kate has been very kind in lending me hers but I must have one of my own and this is to have the monogram put on and be sent home in three days which causes great excitement in our quiet establishment, where every purchase is talked over for months before and after the deed is done. I have sketched it here in order that you may see how fine it will look at my belt with the other golden ornaments waving in the breeze. I have considered the matter ever since I saw them that evening with Laddie, and I have not found them anywhere else, so my mind was made up to-day, and after achieving this purchase I went on and met Rose among the pictures and electrified her with the announcement. After wandering through the endless rooms of the Louvre, . . . and going together to sit for some time before the great picture by Delaroche of Queen Elizabeth, dying in her royal robes, with her courtiers about her, reminding me of Ristori, who copies the picture exactly in her death scene, I then walked home stopping to call at Laddie's on my way. . . . Madame was feeling rather badly at sending her little girls to a Pension near Paris for some years to be educated, as they are learning nothing at home."

On January 25th, Marmee writes in her journal:

"Unexpected pleasure, a letter from May. I try to be satisfied with once a week, but two letters does give me a very refreshing sensation and tones down the blues most astonishingly. She has had a fine time at the 'Healy reception' Miss Peckham accompanies her. She dances first with Mr. Healy, served through the evening with ice cream and *hot* punch. The whole affair very elegant and effective; went home before 12 o'clock, moderate for Paris.

"Mons. Müller praised her Prince 'Timbuctoo' again, and also the head of a fair young woman who sits to their class in the afternoon. She says, 'I have begun to have ideas about pictures and I shall work out something I feel sure if I can take the time for it.' Hopeful and courageous."

Encouraged by the improvement in Mrs. Alcott's health, May writes, suggesting that Louisa come over and join her for the winter:

"I hope the 'Serial' is finished and Lu's head at rest after it. What are her plans and does she still think of Europe as a possibility for this winter? . . . Why not shut up Apple Slump for a year and let Nan have all the pretty things and a general pick, and let Lu come for a year's vacation, if mother continues well and feels she can spare her. I feel now as if I must stay a year or more longer, having proved to my satisfaction that there is enough talent to pay for educating it and giving my life to it. . . . I make plans about a little room for salon and studio, a kitchen and dressing-room, and settling in such a little apartment as a hard-working artist, living for future fame. How should you all like that, for I can better be spared than any of you and could make you an occasional visit of a summer for variety if you wanted me very

much. This is what I think my life must be, if
health and eyes hold out, for I am awfully in
earnest now and can do nothing at home for some
time to come. . . . Next week I may get dis-
couraged and then think strongly of sailing immediately, such being the ups and downs of an
artist life and temperament."

It was not easy for her mother to be reconciled
to the thought of May's prolonging her stay, as
she missed her youngest daughter sadly, but she
concealed her longings, watched for May's letters,
and dwelt with pride on her success. Meanwhile
she followed with interest the Concord doings, and
jotted down occasional items about the various
guests who came to visit them:

"Feb. 1st, 1877. Dr. Dudley of Milwaukee
passes the night here, goes to Emerson's for a
talk in the morning; Sanborn takes tea with him
and they have high talk. The weather was very
fine all the time. He talked about Louisa. I
showed him the pretty hymn she wrote when 13
years of age in her little diary.

'The Kingdom of God is within you.' Mr.
Charles Wendte compiled a small school class-
book and wrote to Louisa for a contribution of
Juvenile poetry; she remembered this, and on

reading it over felt she could do nothing so good now. In her return note to Mr. Wendte, so characteristic, she says: 'I send you a little piece which I found in an old journal of my childhood; coming as it does from a child's heart, while conscious of its weaknesses and its wants, it may touch the heart of other children in like mood'."

A tiny violet pressed, and pasted above an old-fashioned New Year's card such as was used in Europe before the custom became general here, decorates the page, dated February 20th, followed by the words:

"We receive a letter from May with this pretty violet and complimentary card for the New Year. These are interchanged in England and France, as well as visiting cards at the New Year, so delicate. Thank you, my dearest, I wish you many happy and useful years, not length of days, or number of years so desirable to any of us, I think, as usefulness and contentment for,

> Fed from a hidden bowl,
> A lamp burns in my soul
> All days;
> A sacred, secret spark
> Shoots rays."

Two days later, she notes that Louisa has returned after an absence of six weeks in Boston.

"We are glad to get her back amongst us this dreary weather, it creates a new atmosphere in the house, and we all feel more protected when she is about us. She seems quite well and happy. Her success in writing is quite remarkable, and her reputation is made for all future time, as the best writer for young people since Miss Edgeworth and Mrs. Barbauld. She infuses her morals so skillfully and her ethical machinery is so gracefully concealed by the clinging drapery of love, or the thick foliage of events, that her characters blossom out upon you with a new grace and beauty as well as being truthful to the Life.

"Lizzie Bartol and Mrs. Whitman call. Make many inquiries about May and her studies. Louisa takes tea with the Sanborn's."

And at this time May writes entertainingly of her visit to the studio of the famous Couture.

"The great event has been my going with Miss Austin to visit the great painter Couture, and a splendid time we had of it, for in a grubby little street we found the man and family in a dingy room eating their twelve o'clock breakfast. They were most cordial, and Mrs. Couture took us up to the studio where we feasted our eyes on such sketches and pictures as I can hardly give you any idea of, for such strong, true, dashing touches were truly startling, and Miss Austin and I could only gasp out our admiration, which evidently pleased madame immensely, who took as much pleasure in displaying the masterly works of her husband as we did in seeing them.

"They are the best pictures and more to my taste than any I have seen as yet in Paris, and I don't wonder he has the high rank in French art that he does. His great picture in the Luxembourg seems in quite a different style and I do not care so much for it as the smaller ones we saw in his atelier. And he himself is as striking to look at as any of his works, for he has a superb head, broad and massive, with grayish hair, quite thick round his face, fine forehead and eyes, strong nose and mouth but rather a gross chin and jowl, which as a whole, I think, gives a very good and true impression of his character, for with all his genius, he, like so many Frenchmen, has no opinion of women, their goodness, strength, or ability to do anything but bear children and keep house, being created as only a convenience to men.

"So though he encourages pupils who come to him (and pay him $5.00 for seeing him paint), to work, and takes their money, he tells his friends — it is impossible for them ever to paint. Three

American girls are studying with him now but it seems to me a style that can never be taught, being done by inspiration and impossible to repeat, but I considered it a great privilege to have seen what I did, and as we came down from the studio he still sat at breakfast and insisted on chatting pleasantly with us, ending by saying: 'Well ladies, you cannot only say you have seen Couture, but Couture in the bosom of his family,' all of whom rose when we went out, smiling and bowing; one of the two pretty daughters whom I had noticed looked much like her mother, a fair-skinned, dark-eyed woman, buxom and neat, who is said to have taken Couture, rather than he, her. For her father was the concierge of a house owned by Couture, and said to be worth considerable property, so when the old man proposed to the painter to marry his daughter, and offered a handsome *dot* with her, as an important part of the bargain, the latter, with his notions about women, said: 'Yes, she will do as well as any other woman,' and they were married. It is said to have proved a happy marriage for them both, and certainly everything looked so on the day we saw them. Altogether I enjoyed the afternoon trip as much as anything that has happened for a long while, and felt exceedingly obliged to Miss Austin for taking me to see the great lion of

Paris. His pictures are sold before they leave the
easel, at immense prices, though he is rather lazy
and does not paint much besides what he does
before his pupils, as that is his method.

"Now, Marmee dear, I have told you all this
because it greatly interests me and when you see
a picture of his or even in his style, you will see
the kind of painting which I want to do."

Mrs. Alcott's love of Concord with its many
prized memories, especially those connected with
the passing of Beth, is recorded on March 14th,
when she writes:

"Almost twenty years since we returned to Concord, and here we were called to part with our dear
Lizzy. Her dear remains seem to sanctify the
place, and here I wish to be laid, although I often
say it is of little consequence where we are finally
laid in the flesh, for all is dust, and earth must
receive our corruptible part; yet, I must own a
preference to the final resting-place; to rest among
our kindred is a desirable thing to look forward to,
even if we are insensible to the fact. After that the
birds of the air, the dews from heaven, the Stars
above us, even the snows of winter, are beautiful
to contemplate as our companions in their seasons.
The daisies will not forget to smile above me, and

the sweet clouds of heaven moisten their throats with tender rain. Who can fear death and its consequences, if they have repented their sins, hope to be forgiven, and trust all to that power which created, sustained us here, and provides such beauty in the natural world to the end."

A couple of days later she says:

"16th. Anna's birthday, we celebrate it, all she is able to bear, being feeble, with an obstinate cough and cold. A nice letter from May at noon was a pleasant surprise on the occasion. Miss Reed had bought her a Roman Lamp, like this sketch. [Here is inserted May's pen-and-ink drawing of the lamp.] In almost all her letters May has given me some little sketch of the pretty things that are collecting about her in Paris. I save them in this way because I consider this her book, or record of the doings of her Paris excursion. I think she has realized what a sacrifice to me it has been to have her gone so far, and has conscientiously tried to gratify me and her sisters by these frequent and interesting accounts of her progress in Art; the acquaintances she forms, her criticism of famous pictures, her hopes of the future; and regrets that these fine opportunities have come so late in her life."

MAY ALCOTT

The various jottings in Marmee's journal are penned at intervals, which vary according to her state of health, and a month after the last entry she writes:

"May speaks hopefully of the portrait Miss Peckham is doing of her. She says 'it is a likeness which I should wish to be remembered by; as it idealizes my bad points, and it rather exaggerates my good ones, just enough to harmonize the whole *tout ensemble* of her subject.' May has fine lines in her face, the temples remind me of my mother, expressive soft and serene, the mouth heavy and not intellectual. But her character gives a high-born tone, almost grace to the pose of her head, which might be called by some beautiful, wavy hair and much of it. I hope this absence will mature and develop the best traits in her character, improve her health and confirm still further her conviction that her talent for painting needs these further instructions to establish her claims as an Artist of no mean degree. She has worked conscientiously, feeling sure that honest effort will not wholly fail of success."

About this time the family were considering the purchase of the Thoreau House, as a home for Mrs. Pratt and her children, and May's practical mind at once grasped all details of the proposition and she eagerly discussed the project, touching upon both advantages and disadvantages. A little later she writes to her mother enclosing a pen-and-ink sketch of her still-life picture destined to find its way into the Salon:

"Here, dear Marmee, is the still-life group which I have been so busy on the last week, and which everyone praises so much, and in which I feel I have improved so greatly, and learned so much that I am encouraged to take it to Monsieur Müller for criticism. The apples are very yellow and green, with a bright orange in the background, and one in the shadow; then the blue-and-gray jug and straw-colored bottle of Maraschino wine, with its blue label, and metal top, stand on a polished table which reflects the forms enough to be pretty, and as a whole it is a very effective bit of color, as Miss Cassatt said the other morning when she saw it and thought it must be some of Rose's work."

May then speaks of her portrait which, when completed, was sent back to America:

"Next week my portrait is to be done, for I only mean it to be a vigorous study, not a finished picture. Miss Austin and Rose are to do it together and I hope to have both pictures, one of

[179]

which will do for Nan's new house. Ha, ha! I shall have much light blue about me, and have them make me more as I *was* than as I *am*. Then in May, Alice Bartlett shall take it to Marmee as my present. Your spring greeting of March 1st has just come with Lu's and you are certainly good faithful correspondents. I have just sent you two fat envelopes full, so shall try not to send this before Sunday as you will get too expectant with so many in a week, but so many pleasant things come along just now that I can't help scribbling to my Marmee, who I know enjoys reading as much as I do writing them."

It was characteristic of the aspiring artist from Concord to make the most of her opportunities, and much of May's so-called "good luck" was traceable to the alacrity with which she seized upon each chance that came her way, and did her best to guide the "moving finger" which was tracing her line of fate. The following letter, describing her dash back to her lodgings in order to bring her picture to M. Müller's notice, is an admirable example of her ability to travel towards her "luck." She wrote:

"When we got to the studio, we found that it was M. Müller's day for visiting and criticizing.

Then I regretted I had n't known of it and brought my still-life for his opinion, but remembering how few moments it would take to run back and get it, I instantly resolved to do so and let his decision settle my doubts as to its real merit.

"When I got back he was talking with M. Krug in his studio, apart from ours, and I timidly produced my little group of simple objects coming naturally together as they did on our dining-room table. What was my astonishment and perfect delight when he overwhelmed me with praises, saying it was worthy of a pupil of the great still-life painter here (whose name I can't spell), and said he could n't have done it better himself, and that I must send it to the Salon, and he should be proud to have me write myself as his *élève*, or pupil. Krug stood beaming upon me and was pleased at the master's praise, saying, I must at least try and get it exhibited. Müller said: 'Take that into the other studio and show these ladies what, painting simply what you see instead of trying to make a picture, will do even without great practice in color.' Then he looked and looked again, and repeated over and over again, '*Très bien, très bien,* Mlle. Alcott, you cannot do better than go on doing just such things.'

"Was n't that fine? and is n't Marmee as much pleased as her baby over it all? So now I shall have to get it framed and send it in to be criticized by the jury, who will either refuse or accept my humble work. If the former, I shall not be surprised as it's no more than a beginner in oils and a foreigner ought to expect, and it's no disgrace, as 6,000 were refused last year, and if accepted it will be a very great honor, and a fine feather in my cap to start a career with, for color-dealers, picture-purchasers, and all nationalities, turn to the Salon catalogue as the criterion by which to judge of an artist whose name is unknown to them. Next Monday, March 18th, is the day for sending them and a week or more later I shall know about mine. This is all very exciting and Rose and I are nearly worn out with talking and have caught the fever from the artists all about us, who are hurrying for dear life with their work. Hers of Miss d'Alembert makes a very pretty picture."

A visit to a private collection is described with much enthusiasm:

"Today I have been with Kate to a small but most choice collection of pictures which are for sale in a lovely private hotel near us, which belonged to the late rich banker Oppenheim, and since his death, it is open to visitors. I found two exquisite woodland scenes in Diaz' best style. And the portrait of Frederick the Great in hunting costume, by Jérôme; he took the medal of honor on it, it was thought such a *chef d'œuvre*, or shade over, as Lockwood calls it. There is so much action and life in the figure and the whole tells the story so perfectly that I am not surprised that people rave over it. Then four or five of Meissonier's best kept a crowd round them so I could hardly get near enough to see them, though I went early on purpose to have the pictures to myself. Meissonier paints officers and cavaliers in the bright clothes and velvet fixings in the finest style, with the point of a sable brush, every fold, every line of the face, bones of the hand and all details are wonderfully done though on the smallest possible scale. His mounted officers are thought surprisingly good and bring immense prices, for the horses are such living creatures with every hair laid to make the glossy whole; a bay mare, which almost always makes a striking feature in the foreground, particularly touches my heart, I leave you to guess why. A splendid large water-color by Fortuny was not to be overlooked among the other gems, nor a fine Troyon, of cattle and geese driven by an old Frenchwoman with a bright handkerchief on her head. Altogether, I have hardly enjoyed any collection so entirely as this, for though small it is selected with infinite taste, and the whole house shows great refinement in its perfect appointments. Tapestries, Japanese work, fine china, bronzes, beautiful colors in satin furniture, make it a place to linger in, I assure you."

As the date for the exhibition approached, the excitement among the art students increased and May's letters reflected the intensity of feeling experienced by the throng waiting for the portals to swing open:

"We live in exciting times, for on Saturday the great rush began toward the great Palais de l'Industrie, and pictures appeared in every direction; enormous nudes elegantly framed, small sketches, water-colors carried by the ladies themselves, immense furniture wagons packed tight stood in lines before the great entrance. This state of things continues for three days, when the intense excitement culminates, from five to six o'clock on the last day, for exactly at six, the great doors are shut and the officials are inexorable. You may imagine our anxiety when Rose, who being disappointed in the d'Alembert portrait, had begun one of me which promised to be so striking a picture that at the eleventh hour she decided to send mine instead of the d'Alembert, if by a miracle she could paint it in time, and so told the man not to come for it till the latest possible moment.

"At eight o'clock Monday, I began to pose in my blue dress with wide frill in the pointed neck, and a blue turned-up hat over my hair in thick curls and crimps, falling gracefully on neck and shoulders. I never moved, but to drink some tea, all day, while Rose painted at lightning pace, and Miss Austin joined in making a sketch. We had the greatest fun, particularly as I kept dictating, when they came to the various features, to make the mouth smaller, the chin shorter, the eyes longer, etc. At last darkness descended about six o'clock and stopped our labors, when a general review of the day's work began and was pronounced *remarkably fine*, for a gush of blue with my hair, you know, was always most charming and the whole thing has an old-fashioned picturesqueness. On Tuesday the same scene was repeated in our little studio, the sitting being only relieved by a jolly breakfast of eggs, fried potatoes, coffee and jelly-cake. Miss Austin ate with us, and such a merry artistic set was never seen before, I flourishing around in my swirling blue robes, with my hair tumbling down my back to below my waist, much to their entertainment. We were all wrought up to the last pitch as it neared the time for the picture to be sent for, and at last we had to give up sending mine as it was too unfinished, though much more striking than Miss d'Alembert's, which reluctantly we put into the very splendid frame Rose had bought for it, and the men bore it away with Lockwood's, framed in gold and black, also my little still-life in a cheap but pretty, unpretentious frame costing ten francs, or $2. For I decided to try my luck as everyone advised me to do so, it being a great thing if it was accepted, and no disgrace if it was n't.

"Kate had already gone to see the fun at the Palace de l'Industrie and returned later telling us that at ten minutes of six o'clock our pictures had not arrived, but that an immense crowd was there, among them a great number of art students, who as the pictures were carried up the flights of stairs and dumped down to be registered, sent off howls of praise or blame, and cries of admiration at the work of any known master like Jérôme, or Bonnat. She said, as it neared six o'clock and still wagon after wagon-load drove up to be unloaded, the porters got perfectly wild and just rushed the pictures in and up like mad, the elegant frames flying in splinters, sometimes amid the jeers of the crowd, or groans of the poor artist, who saw his treasured work treated thus rudely.

"Kate stood three hours without being aware of time, it was so exciting, and not seeing ours arrive she, at just the last moment, went into the street, to find our wagon just driving up, the last of six yet to be unloaded, and as she stopped to hurry the men, out came the portrait of Miss d'Alembert, looking finely, she said, among the other varieties of good, bad and indifferent. The crowd was so great she could n't wait to see if the others got out on time, but as they have n't been brought back to us today, we hope they are all safely in. When we here at home had seen our precious works-of-art descend the stairs, we returned to the studio, there to fall into our chairs perfectly exhausted with the fuss, Rose going to bed worn out, thinking that a nap was the only thing that would rest her overstrained nerves. Miss Austin painted away the rest of the A.M. on her portrait of me, which is so masterly in parts that, as the face does n't suit her, she asks the favor of me to sit to her and a friend (in their private studio up by the Arc de Triomphe) again, in a week or two. This, of course, I shall like to do, particularly as she will give me the picture, when done, which will be immensely valuable, as she hardly knows her power yet, but must soon be appreciated and will put her name among the first of our artists. She is a pupil of Hunt's, and her style is more like his than any one else that I can think of, only a little bolder if anything perhaps.

"I find it very interesting to see how I look to other people and am surprised that they succeed in making such pleasing, effective pictures of such a plain woman. Rose acknowledged that she hardly suspected what picturesque material was to be found in this oldish girl dressed in plain black all the time, and that a bit of blue and a dashing hat, with a curl or two waving in the breeze, entirely transformed me. Now enough about me and my portrait, but as it has proved of such absorbing interest, I could n't help dilating on its charms, and send a sketch that Marmee can see what she is going to have to remind her of her big baby, who can't return to her arms, quite yet, so sends this idealized representative."

The fate of May's little still-life picture, for the success of which she did not dare to hope, was finally decided, and Marmee's journal for April, 1877, closes with the record of her daughter's artistic triumph in having her work admitted to the Salon.

"April 21st. Memorable news from Paris. May's picture admitted to the great 'Art Exhibition' of the season. A small-sized group of 'Fruit and Bottles', with an inexpensive frame, so the merit was all in the painting, the work."

In response to this good news, May received a letter of congratulation from her father, penned in red ink, which, he asserted, "is the color that best represents your success at the Salon." He continues:

"So I begin my note of salutation to you. It is an honor to yourself and to us all: the whole household joined in their chorus at the happy news. . . . Your star is still in the ascendant and only yourself can dim its lustre. Every one to whom your success has been mentioned has taken pride in your honors. . . . Louisa's new story in the *No Name* series comes out tomorrow. If you know its title, you are better informed than I am. I am told by your mother that it surpasses its predecessors in power and brilliancy, and that the author will not be casually recognized by its readers. Louisa, like yourself, appears to be adding to the honors to her name and what is far better, giving pleasure and nobler views of life to her million readers and admirers."

MAY ALCOTT

The above suggestion concerning Louisa's new book ("A Modern Mephistopheles") points to the fact that it was to her mother rather than to her scholarly father that this daughter turned for criticism of her forthcoming work; even as May, winning her laurels in the art world, turned instinctively to lay them before Marmee's shrine.

CHAPTER VIII

The Salon of 1877

THE Palais de l'Industrie, in which was housed the Salon of 1877, was a relic of an earlier Exposition Universelle, and it was later swept away, to be replaced by a far more ornate structure, built for the Exposition of 1900. It stood on the Champs Élysées, and a door at one end of the building, nearest the Arc de Triomphe, was assigned to the reception of pictures submitted for the Salon. These, as has been stated, were rapidly unloaded from large vans which were drawn up before this entrance, laden with canvases precious in the eyes of their producers, no matter how worthless they might be pronounced by the ruthless committee. Some of the canvases were so large as to require the aid of eight or ten workmen to handle them, and meanwhile, the groups of onlookers would exercise their privilege of free speech, commenting frankly upon the pictures being borne up the steps. At nightfall, the critical mob of art students, hoarse and weary, wended its homeward way, to undergo the cruel six weeks of suspense that must elapse before the rendering of the verdict by the jury.

And for May Alcott, this suspense ended in surprise and delight. Her little *still-life*, for the success of which she had slight hopes, was accepted and admirably hung, while the work of her friend, Rose Peckham, who had been working for a much longer period in Paris, was rejected. A bitter disappointment for the three friends.

A gleeful communication from May, headed "Joy, joy, joy", is annotated with the words "Salon letter, April 18th" (a lucky Concord Day!). And it recounts the acceptance of the picture previously described:

"My dear Marmee's heart will be delighted to hear that my little picture is accepted at the great Salon exhibition, where from 8500 works sent in, only 2000 were accepted, and mine was thought worthy a place among the best. Who would have imagined such good fortune, and so strong a proof that Lu does not monopolize all the Alcott talent. Ha! ha! sister, this is the first feather plucked from your cap, and I shall endeavor to fill mine with so many waving in the breeze that you will be quite ready to lay down your pen and rest on your laurels already won. Mine was such a simple unpretending little study, plainly framed and without any influence at court to help me in with it, that I do feel it a great compliment to have it stand on its own merit as it does. It won't look bigger than a postage-stamp when hung among so many immense pictures, in such large halls, but on its account I have a free pass to go as often as I please and take in my friends, which is convenient to say the least. So sing for joy, dear Marmee, and be proud of your ugly duckling, won't you?

"The sad part of the whole thing is that both of Rose's portraits are *refused*, which is a terrible disappointment, for both the sisters have had but this one thought for the last year, and Rose has worked for it steadily and conscientiously with Monsieur Lefebre, to criticise everything she did, and help her with his influence, as he was one of the jury to decide the merits of each. So this morning when she brought the news of their refusal it was too much for both of them, and I took their grief so to heart as to almost forget my own happy surprise.

"If Rose could only have got my portrait finished in time, it would have been sure of being accepted, and have done her more credit than either of the others.[1] Yesterday I got a pretty, cheap frame for it, and now it stands on an antique chair at

[1] The year following this refusal saw Rose Peckham's portrait, which was submitted to the Salon, accepted by the jury and "hung on the line."

my elbow looking so fine that I long to know what you will say to it, and I wish I could put it right into your hands myself. . . .

"I send a good-night kiss, dear Marmee, with this to warm your heart.

MAY

Among those bitterly disappointed by the refusal of their work was the painter Moss, whose studio May had already described. Of the fate of his picture she wrote:

"Eve, I told you about sometime ago (by Moss), is also refused, tho' he sent two works, and he goes home to Philadelphia this summer; he has worked hard for more than a year, spending a great deal of money on models, in hopes to gain this one taste of success and now has failed. It is dreadfully discouraging and artists sometimes even commit suicide at such a result, but these are foolish Frenchmen, who do it at the least provocation. You see I tell you all these items that you may step into this little Art world here and appreciate this compliment to a humble Concordian. Miss Cassatt has two refused also, which is more strange than its happening to Rose, as the former's work is exceedingly strong and fine, but perhaps it's too original a style for these fogies to appreciate."

(It was after this refusal of Miss Cassatt's work at the Salon that Degas persuaded her to send no more of her pictures there but to exhibit instead with the friends of the Impressionist school. This she did, at once recognizing Manet, Courbet, and Degas as her masters although they represented the revolutionary school of that day.)

Among the most notable pieces of sculpture exhibited at this Salon was Rodin's famous "Man of the Bronze Age", a work destined to bring its creator fame as a great sculptor. The previous year had seen the final acceptance of his "Man With a Broken Nose", which had been refused almost a decade earlier, and its successor, typifying the "Age of Bronze", was at this time tucked away in an obscure nook. However, just before the opening of the Salon of '77, a group of sculptors gathered about this figure, hardly visible in one of the darkest corners of a section playfully called "the Morgue", and murmurs of admiration were followed by a storm of indignation directed towards the committee which had placed this masterpiece in so poor a setting.

Whose work was this?

The name Rodin was unknown to the group of sculptors gathered about the statue, but at last some one cried, "I know, he is a fellow who works as an assistant for Carrière-Belleuse; he had a very remarkable bust, a man with a broken nose, in the Salon a year ago." After discussing the work with increasing enthusiasm the protest was loudly voiced and a riotous scene ensued; the guardians were sought and before long Rodin's figure was placed in an admirable position. When the Salon opened a critical war raged about this statue, which detractors declared was made of casts from nature; the charge, however, was promptly disproved and from this attack Rodin came forth triumphant, an acknowledged master.

The Salon of '77 also displayed an interesting portrait of a young American prima donna who had taken Paris by storm, Emma La Jeunesse, a Canadian by birth, who was helping to extend the fame of her home city, Albany, New York. Mlle. Albani's praises were being sung all over Paris at this time, and especially had she triumphed in the rôle of "Lucia di Lammermoor."

Then it was that young Will Low, who, with his friend Robert Louis Stevenson, had fallen under the spell of her voice, decided upon a daring venture. He would ask the great singer to sit to him for her portrait, pleading the privilege of a fellow townsman, as he also hailed from Albany. Low boldly approached the prima donna, whose heart melted under his admiring protestations and who having acceded to his request, with unfailing patience crossed the city many times to reach his studio, which was sometimes far from comfortable, risking her health to do so. Indeed upon a certain day when the fire went out, she contracted a severe cold and almost closed the Paris Opera House in consequence. The report of Low's success spread among the art students, who would by seeming accident line the path to the singer's carriage, envying the lucky fellow student who was gallantly escorting her to her vehicle. This admiration was later expressed in the presentation of an album of original sketches which, as Mr. Low has stated, contained the work of every American art student in Paris at that time. Low's portrait of Albani, as "Lucia", is now in the possession of the Albany Club, at Albany, New York.

It was just at this time that Saint-Gaudens modeled in Paris the exquisite reredos for St. Thomas' Church, New York, which was afterward destroyed by fire; this work was then under way, and young Low, who had come to share Saint-Gaudens' studio, watched its growth with enthusiasm.

Following the opening of the Salon, May penned a graphic picture of this dramatic spectacle:

[197]

MAY ALCOTT

My dear old Lu, — The excitement of Varnishing Day is over and I must describe it as well as possible to you who love the artistic side of Paris life so much. All the night before I was most restless concerning the eventful Monday, when I was to see my work hung among the gorgeous great pictures by the first French painters. So at early dawn I waked to find a superbly bright day and satisfied on this point, I tried to sleep again till seven o'clock came, when I half dressed and putting on my wrapper virtuously did up the dinner things left in confusion, the night before. Being carefully robed in our evening clothes we did n't feel like cleaning pots and pans in our little kitchen. Then at nine o'clock, after having a good hot bowl of chocolate, I descended to meet Mr. Parish and settling ourselves in a little open carriage we drove off to the Palais l'Industrie and mounting the broad stairs stood face to face in the first big salon, with my study of still-life. It looked very small amid the enormous ones which surrounded it on all sides, but it held its own surprisingly well being good, strong, vigorous painting, simple in its subject and unaffectedly treated. The great frames round it made a superb edge of gold making the neat little frame look like a mere inner panel and proved most becoming. Besides this fortunate circumstance, the hanging committee did me the honor to put it so low as to be almost "on the line", as those just in range of the eye are called, and artists sometimes pay large bribes to the managers to get theirs put on this line. When I saw what fine specimens of still-life there were there I was surprised that mine was accepted, for these French students paint most elaborately arranged eastern stuffs, Venetian glass, brass, armor, on an immense scale, and give much time to it, finishing up every detail most perfectly. So I came to the conclusion that the very simplicity of mine must have been its great merit, though Müller assured me it would without fail be accepted when he saw it. Well, after contemplating my picture and the looks of my name on the second page of the fat catalogue, arranged alphabetically, we passed on to find thirty rooms full of paintings, beside long galleries of water-colors, etchings, engravings and designs, while below in a glass-covered garden stood the accepted sculptures, tastefully arranged near the great restaurant filled with hungry visitors. Parish is a handsome blond fellow, most elegant and gentlemanly in appearance so I aired my best plumage even to petticoats and boots, yellow gloves with four buttons, etc., meeting all the artists, Bridgman, Blashfield, Moss, Ramsey and

the crowd generally, as we call them. All stopped
to congratulate me on my picture and its hanging,
and Mitchell came to chat about his etching,
Leland and others payed their respects. . . .

After this I stumbled on Bigot and Madame,
and then a fleeting recognition to Lippincott, Miss
Gadsall, and some studio inmates, feeling quite at
home in this great crowd and rather alarmed to
find how many people I already knew there. A
great Madonna by Bouguereau, a portrait of
Thiers by Bonnat, Bridgman's "Egyptian Burial
at Sea", which was finely hung and looked like a
different thing from what it did at the private
opening, I noticed particularly.

Bacon has a good picture in the Salon, and you
would be surprised to see how many Bostonians,
Philadelphians and New Yorkers' names figure in
the catalogue, which I will forward to you after
the exhibition closes, as Marmee will like to see
her baby's name combining the *May* and *Alcott*
both in French print. Just as Parish, who leaves
for London to-night and was much hurried of
course, was saying good-bye at the Palais today,
Mr. Ramsey advanced and asked me to share his
cab with him home, so we drove gaily home after
a most successful entrée at the Salon. The next
day I took Fanny Lombard, dressed in her fine

new suit, and we had a jolly time together, taking
our lunch in the restaurant. We saw the pictures
before the crowd came in, or rather got some notion of the most important ones, and then after
lunch took another general survey, of both the
water-color room and the collection of designs,
etchings, etc., then finished up by studying the
toilettes, as the fashionables crowded in towards
night. Some of them were quite fine but we
decided that at the New York exhibitions, or even
the Art Club rooms [Boston], one saw *more* dress
and more taste in costumes than even in Paris at
the Salon. They say that the great houses like
Worth and Pingat make an entirely different
class of costumes, more rich and expensive for
exporting to American markets than any for sale
in Paris, and you all get the fashions sooner
through *Harper's Bazar*, and those fashion-books,
than we do, unless an American goes into much
society here.

But seeing well-dressed people convinced me I
must buy a bonnet, as my hat did well enough for
every day, being exceedingly becoming, but that
I must have something to wear to be a little gayer
sometimes, so off I posted, after leaving Fanny,
to the Temple and bought a blue bonnet such as I
have always had, and after all that color is more

becoming than any other and goes with brown and black so prettily, and now with a light veil tied over it the whole thing is more useful than a yellow straw; which is very fashionable but only useful for one season, and then has to be thrown away. Capot shape is much worn now like this [small sketch inserted] with very little trimming, perhaps a bit of black velvet and a bunch of yellow flowers.

May's success, with her detailed descriptions of the Salon, awakened much enthusiasm in the little home circle, and many letters of congratulation fluttered across to Paris.

Upon April 23, she writes in response to the family congratulations, expressing her happiness at being able to please them, and her hope that sometime she may also be able to aid them by her art productions. She cautions them, however, not to expect too much, as she may "flat out" in the end, and she protests that she thinks more of pleasing "Marmee" than anything else, and will send home her salon picture at the earliest opportunity for Annie to hang in her dining room.

She comments with amusement on some suggestion proffered about her work, remarking:

"I roared over the charmingly assured tone of Lu's saying 'Don't paint in Millet's later style', as if I could ever paint in any style like his, and if the Shaw collection is still at the Boston Athenæum, be sure to go to see his 'Sower', which Mr. Emerson calls the great picture of the world. Millet is dead, you know, and among the other great names are Corot, Fromentin, and Diaz, who have died lately and left no one capable of filling their places."

May's admonition to the family regarding their attitude towards Millet recalls the fact that as a pupil of William Morris Hunt she had undoubtedly acquired an enthusiasm for this French master's work long before reaching Europe, for in Hunt's studio a fine collection of the Frenchman's pictures had been displayed. Hunt's classes, which he carried on in Boston in the Mercantile Building for three years, were eagerly attended, and probably no other city in America at this period offered such advanced modern instruction as did Boston. After three years, however, Hunt found that his own work was suffering, and he arranged to have one of his pupils, Miss Helen M. Knowlton, carry on the classes, he himself coming in merely to criticize and to correct the work. During this period Miss Knowlton took careful notes of Hunt's talks to his classes, for her own use in teaching; these notes were later published in book form as "Hunt's Talks on Art", a work familiar to all art students.

In the great Boston fire in 1872, Hunt's studio was destroyed, and in addition to the loss of his own pictures, five canvases by Millet went up in flames, as did those of several other French masters. It was indeed most fortunate that shortly before this time, five of Millet's works had been purchased by Mr. Quincy A. Shaw, who, for ten thousand dollars, secured "The Sower", "The Shepherdess", "The Shepherd in the Moonlight", "Sheep Shearers", and "The Digger."

Boston, which prides itself to-day on the possession of so many of the pictures of the French master, was slow to awaken to their merit, and the lack of appreciation shown at the exhibition held at the Boston Athenæum, to which May Alcott refers in her letter, awoke in Hunt great indignation. This exhibition, which included paintings by Millet, Rousseau, and Troyon, was severely criticized by the head of the Art Department at Harvard University, to whom Hunt replied in the *Boston Advertiser*, declaring that the standard at Harvard had indeed reached a dizzy height when the work of Millet was ranked as "trivial."

As has been already suggested, Hunt was also a great admirer of Turner, whose work had taken a strong hold on his fancy, so that he used to say: "The Turners follow me! I cannot get away from them. They are all that I can hold." And one may rest assured that few pupils of Hunt failed to appreciate the work of either the French or the English master previously referred to.

With the excitement of the Salon over, May Alcott began to think of country scenes and of the opportunities for sketching out of doors. She wrote:

"I long to get into the country and try my hand at a bit of nature with the new ideas I have been simmering to help me along. I don't want to paint merely portraits, which for money is a dog's life, but old donkey-women with yellow handkerchiefs on their heads, pretty children on the queer stone steps of some of the quaint houses of Brittany, perhaps, and such things, where landscape and figures combine to make a pleasing whole, and if I find what I want I shall stay all winter perhaps, out of Paris making pictures, though probably I shall find it necessary to study drawing much longer. Sometimes it does seem such an endless task to try to learn all that a painter must know before he attempts pictures."

MAY ALCOTT

It may be amusing to record May's description of a Paris gown in 1877:

"You will like to know that my new black silk came home last night cut 'Princess', all in one, laced up the back and tight as possible over the hips, making me a superb figure, the P's say, and it is a simple but exceedingly stylish dress, with a graceful train and handsomely finished in detail, only trimmed with the wide piece of heavy silk fringe across the front breadth which is folded like a scarf, draped across the front, to break the severe outline, and three fine silk plaitings all round the bottom of the front and sides, ending in one just at the train. I shall get some real black lace and quill round the neck, with crêpe-lèse inside, and it will be just what I want for the studio-party if they give one, for the Mannings, as Mr. Ramsey spoke of doing. I cut the blue waterproof myself by a pattern into a polonaise and it sets surprisingly well; so much so, that the P's say they shall do theirs just so. It is basted ready, with my new underwaist, which I have also cut out for myself, for the machine, when Miss Reade brings it from London, as Warner is to send it by her to save duties which are high on such things between the two countries. I shall get a big hat and sketching umbrella and then shall feel ready for the country. It would delight your eyes, all of you, to see my head look as it used to with a little roll on the top and my new yellow comb, and three fat curls dropping off at the back, the front all wavy and thick so that on the whole it quite transforms me and I look more like my portrait than you imagine."

She also describes the purchase of a stuffed owl which served later as a model for one of her best still-life pictures, later accepted at the Salon of 1879:

"The other day, coming from the Atelier, I saw some fine stuffed birds in an old auction room filled with old rubbish, and picked from the rest a fine owl, large, round-eyed and solemn looking, with creamy feathers, shading brown on the wings, which are so pretty that if I did n't want to paint him I should tweak one of them off for my hat. The joke of the whole thing is that as the man stood at the door, I said, 'How much for the owl?' expecting he would say at least 12 or 15 francs, as Alice paid the latter price for one not half so handsome; so you will appreciate my quick wit, when he said '2 francs' and I quickly responded 'I will give you 1½ francs for it,' whereupon he clapped a paper round it and I bore it home, for all to admire not only the noble bird, but the shrewdness displayed in my bargain. Alice is furious at it all, and the Mannings all admire it, also the Peckhams to such an extent that I bought a hawk at the same place for Rose as a present."

A description of her visit to Healy's studio is very entertaining:

"I have been busy on a still-life of a jug and paint-brushes, a paint-box half open, and a little bottle of varnish, all standing on my bright rug for a bit of color, and Rose says it is finely done, and an improvement on my Salon one. This quite contents me as all I expect is to improve from one to another.

"Thursday being Healy day I went to the house and was taken by the daughter across their yard to find Ma and Pa, a regular Darby and Joan, in the Studio enjoying a look at his great portrait of Bismarck, which he has been in Germany three weeks to paint. He was splendidly entertained and has succeeded to the great satisfaction of the Bismarck family in making a strikingly lifelike and vigorous picture of a very ugly man. The lower part of his face is redeemed somewhat by a very high forehead and he has a grand figure, broad shouldered and well proportioned. He is six feet three inches when standing, but Healy has taken him sitting by a table with one arm leaning on it, while the other holds a quill pen, and the eyes are slightly raised, with the head thrown back in order to show his eyes, as all the flabby overhanging brows and masses of fat would otherwise almost entirely hide them. It is cleverly done and certainly Healy has more perfect facility with the brush than any one I ever saw, which is something, though the immortal fire is entirely left out of his work. I had an artistic call and then hurried home, for this is such April weather that half a dozen little showers descend in an afternoon and are inconvenient when one is in calling array."

May's repeated suggestions that Louisa join her in Paris awaken a hearty response in the other's breast, but she feels that she must remain in Concord, though from time to time she voices her desire for a change of scene and pens an amusing description of the prosaic surroundings which contrast vividly with those of Paris. To such a communication May replies:

"Your description of the view from my window with Gray trotting by while a draggle-tailed dog is rooting in the garden, convulsed me, as I know it so well having seen all phases of Concord scenery for so many years. . . . I wish more than you do, dear Lu, that you were here, and as I walked alone to the Arc de Triomphe this springy afternoon, through the lovely Parc Monceaux filled with children, their *bonnes*, elegant equipages, and the picturesque ruins, which though really new are such good imitations of old pillars, bridges etc., that the effect is lovely, how I wished we could have gone in sisterhood."

As the season advances she writes:

"We have been having very warm weather here and my blue cambric came out today for the first time. Sunday morning Kate began the day by reading a chapter in father's book, while Rose reclined on the couch and I sewed. It sounded sweet and refreshing and we voted it most wholesome reading. For a few days Rose has been quite tired and ailing and I think if Grez proves a success after I have been there a week or so, they may join me there before going to Switzerland."

CHAPTER IX

The Magic Circle at Grez

DURING the spring of 1877, May Alcott's letters told of her plan to spend the summer months at Grez, a charming little hamlet which was at just that period becoming a Mecca for art students. That she succeeded in carrying out this project seems probable, although it is uncertain how long she stayed there, as her home correspondence during this summer seems to have vanished, and her communications during the following autumn suggest that her sojourn in this artist's paradise was brief. Yet she speaks of it with enthusiasm in her little "guide" for art students, describing its location as "within walking distance from Barbizon", and but a "donkey-ride from Fontainebleau", while she praises its picturesque beauty, and freedom from all needless conventions, which has won for it growing popularity. She writes of its primitive life:

"One painter after another, with mind filled by many lingering doubts as to what it would be like, has ventured to go, generally being received on his arrival by all the inhabitants of the town, who turn out to see each newcomer and divide any luggage among themselves, for transportation to the little Inn, which until this year has been the only accommodation afforded. The place has its old bridge, its boating and bathing, the river making these possible for ladies as well as gentlemen, flannel-shirts and tramp dresses being the order of the day. Fine clothes are out of place and strictly forbidden the freedom-loving set which now annually meets in the small rooms of the 'auberge', where board was from four to five francs a day."

She closes her remarks about the place with the reflection that Grez in some ways is a reminder of Clark's Island, off Plymouth, Massachusetts, for while the latter is by the sea, both places possess a similar charm for those "who have once been adventurous enough to spend a summer there."

The evidence at hand points quite conclusively to the fact that in the summer of 1877, May's lucky star guided her to this little town to share for a brief period the life of this art colony whose members were destined to play important parts in the artistic world.

Two years before this time, the possibilities of Grez had been discovered by Will H. Low, of New

York, who, with other art students had been making the far-famed Barbizon his summer workshop, and on his recommendation a small group migrated to found another center of artistic activity, only a short distance from their previous *habitat*, beloved by painters for half a century.

When in 1849, Jean François Millet went to Barbizon for a summer holiday, and there remained because living was cheap and the place healthful, and also because he could find there models on which to build his own ideal of art, the place had long been a summer resort for painters, and its small Inn an artists' rendezvous. Indeed, a quarter of a century before the coming of Millet, the fame of Barbizon had been established, in 1824, by Claude Aligny, and Philippe Le Dieu. These two painters, who had wandered down to Fontainebleau to visit a friend in a porcelain manufactory, started out for some woodland sketching and lost their way in the depths of the forest. As night shut down upon them, they gratefully accepted the offer of a shepherd, who led them to Barbizon, o'er which, perchance, the painter's star was hovering, and hospitably allowed them to sleep upon the straw within his sheepfold. The following morning found them enchanted with the beauty of the place, and they remained for prolonged sketching, later returning after spreading the news of their discovery among their friends. Then others came, and in the year 1830 a hotel was established and filled with painters, soon to make Barbizon world-famous, for the list of habitués came to include Corot, Rousseau, Diaz, Dupré, Barye, and finally Millet, and during the next forty years, all French artists of note, and others from all parts of the world, found their way thither.

And it was there that Will Low and his friend Wyatt Eaton were happily associated with Millet during his final years, and from this much-prized friendship with the master, brought back to their own country standards of art and a new inspiration that were to bring about the founding of the Society of American Artists.

It was a Boston painter, William Babcock, then living in France, who was the first American to appreciate Jean François Millet. In 1866, he took William Morris Hunt to Millet's studio at Barbizon, and introduced him to the master, whose genius was at once recognized by the American painter. The "Sheep-Shearers" at this time stood on the Frenchman's easel, and Hunt inquired if it were sold. To this Millet responded that it was to be taken in payment for a long-delayed color bill. Hunt promptly paid this bill and bought the picture, later purchasing many other works, so that eventually he came to own at least a dozen of this master's paintings.

Two years before May Alcott's association with Grez, the little group of American painters at Barbizon had been growing restive for lack of proper exercise for limbs as well as brushes, and then it was that young Will Low had told of the beauties of the little hamlet upon the other side of the forest of Fontainebleau, adjacent to the river, which might furnish them with much-desired exercise, as well as opportunities for boating and bathing, unknown at Barbizon. With one accord the little group cried out that they would go at once to view this lovely spot where they might row and swim, declaring that they were weary of "washing in a bowl no larger than a tea-cup."

Forthwith, a party of six, which included "Bob" Stevenson and his cousin Robert Louis Stevenson, from Scotland, set off across the forest, and after a twenty-mile drive, drew up at Chevillon's, the little inn, which later became a center for art students. The following year, Barbizon was abandoned for Grez, and 1876, the summer preceding May Alcott's coming, found the Anglo-Saxons in full possession of the quaint inn, where among the prime enthusiasts were the Stevenson cousins, who had in Edinburgh shared so many light-hearted pranks together.

Robert Alan Mowbray Stevenson, who later became Professor of Fine Arts at Liverpool University, was by all his friends considered the more brilliant of the two, being famed for his wit and his extraordinary conversational gift, though he possessed less power of concentration than his kinsman. "Bob" was at this time studying at the atelier of Carolus Duran, in Paris, and there Robert Louis Stevenson had joined him in search of change and rest, being somewhat out of health; and with the coming of the summer season, he followed his cousin to Barbizon, and on to Grez.

And at this point one may well pause to reflect for a brief space upon the part that Grez played in the life of Robert Louis Stevenson, furnishing as it did, in 1876, the "time, and the place, and the loved one altogether", for here it was that this distinguished writer met his fate. In his essay entitled "Forest Notes", he has painted a charming word-picture of the summer life lived at that time. In the fall of this crucial year, Low made a sketch of him, which shows that at this period his hair was light in color, a fact that has been ques-

tioned by those who have described it as quite
dark, its color in later years.

In speaking of him at this period, Low says:
"The charm of his presence was both appealing
and imperative"; and picturing their days of happy
companionship, he describes the "long afternoons
spent with him in the woods, his book thrown aside,
the long fingers twisting cigarettes of thread-like
dimensions," declaring, "I have never known one
roll so thin a cigarette as Stevenson, and the
constant flow of talk and interchange of thought
come back to me like the opening chapters of a
book, which one has perused with increasing delight, only to find it at the end 'by a wilful con-
vulsion of nature, finished too soon.' "

At this time, while the others worked industriously at their painting, "Louis" Stevenson was
apparently idle, and it was not until later that his
friends realized through what a formative period
in his work he was passing. But those who knew
him then found afterwards in his works many
ideas, reflections, incidents and phrases born in
those idle summer days, when he was storing the
treasure-house of his mind and accumulating material that was to reappear later in new and
delightful dress.

Undoubtedly his life in this community played

no small part in Stevenson's subsequent work, and he has described Grez in his essay entitled "Fontainebleau" as a merry place after its kind; pretty to see, merry to inhabit; while a picture of his cousin "Bob" may be recognized in his article on "Talk and Talkers." Grez appears as the home of Doctor Desprez, and it was there that Stevenson evolved the idea of a barge project for traveling in many directions by river, a dream that was never realized save in his story of an "Inland Voyage." Yet this plan was launched, and almost carried out during the summer of 1877, when the star of May Alcott crossed the path of many others destined to shine more brightly than her own in the field of art, though all were aiding the great cause dear to each painter's heart.

At the quaint little inn close to the river, Stevenson, who declared that there was much that made life on land undesirable, busied himself with studying maps and laying out river routes in all directions for inland travel; a barge was purchased and its ownership vested in the two Stevensons and their friends Enfield and Simpson. Great plans were made; the craft was to be decorated and arranged with lounging rooms and a studio. The owners would go south in winter, returning by slow degrees, and finally reaching Paris in time to moor their barge not far from the doors of the Salon, which would receive their works.

The craft, having been purchased, was taken to a near-by river town where the leading carpenter was set to work upon her; she was christened *The Eleven Thousand Virgins of Cologne*, and lay for some months in the river near the ancient town of Moret. But from this place she never started on her adventurous career; and her eventual fate was described by Stevenson: "She rotted in the stream where she was beautified. She felt not the impulse of the breeze; she was never harnessed to the patient track-horse." And she was finally sold in order to defray the owners' indebtedness to the indignant carpenter of Moret.

Among those who were numbered as May Alcott's friends, during this period, was one whose presence at Grez has been already foreshadowed, and whose striking personality and powers of fascination were soon to bring her into world-wide notice, Mrs. Osbourne. She and May Alcott spent many hours together at Julien's studio, but whether their first meeting place was in this atelier or in the little colony at Grez one cannot say. It is, however, certain that this notable figure, with her dark beauty, was summering at Grez in 1877, her second season there.

When the first group of artists invaded the picturesque hamlet, astounding the rural population by their alien customs and above all by their unprecedented love of water, the small community was quite exclusively a masculine possession. Free from all small conventions or restraining social customs, the newcomers strode about the village attired in bathing trunks and sandals, perpetually on their way for a swim in the river, where the canoes rapidly multiplied and where tub-races soon became popular. At first the rural population stood quite aghast at the aquatic innovations, but ere long they learned to accept the new régime complacently, as they did the increase in trade.

Then into this masculine community in 1876 came two engaging but unwelcome feminine figures. They were mother and daughter, art students and Californians. The elder had vivid eyes that gleamed from under a mass of dark hair, while the younger, of more robust type, was equally attractive. At the time of their coming Louis Stevenson was absent from the circle at Grez, but after some scrutiny they were welcomed by "Bob", as having proved themselves to be "the right sort", and worthy of admission to this Painters' Paradise. But when this feminine invasion was reported to Louis Stevenson, who was then in Paris, he recoiled in comic disgust at the suggestion, exclaiming, "It's the beginning of the end", little suspecting the truth of his own prophecy.

A little later, Louis returned to Grez, and the spell was upon him, and ere long it was evident to his friends that his feeling for Mrs. Osbourne was no mere passing fancy. With Stevenson it was indeed the beginning of a tie that was to end only with his life.

In the process of gathering up the threads that lead back to those art-student days at Grez, it has seemed of interest to communicate with Mr. Will H. Low, whose success, both as an artist and as a literary craftsman, are too well known to need further comment.

In reply to the question "Did you meet May Alcott in the summer of 1877, at Grez?" the answer came in the negative, accompanied by the expression of much regret that the writer had missed numerous Concord associations with which he had been on the point of coming in close touch. His letter may well be included in this chapter, as he belongs in this the "Magic Circle."

Mr. Low writes that in 1877 he was only at Grez a couple of times, and he did not meet Miss

Alcott, a fact he much deplores, as he likes well to be identified with Concord, although, strange to say, he has never been there. He asserts:

For many generations my people on my mother's side lived there. My grandmother Betsy Buttrick emigrated to Albany at the behest of Samuel Steele, my grandfather. She was a niece of the Major, who commanded "the shot heard round the world", and when later I was trying hard to cast the skin of serpent-like France, at Nantucket, my friend Frank Lathrop, who was living with his brother in the "Manse", at Concord, invited me to spend a week with him, — and I did n't go.

I have a still closer tie, for my (second) wife, Mary Fairchild's sister Florence, married a son of W. T. Harris, who succeeded Bronson Alcott as the head of the School of Philosophy, and was living in the Old Orchard House; she visited her sister there for the summer of 1880 and 1882, and occupied May Alcott's room; she has often described to me the copies of Flaxman's designs which ornamented the woodwork. Being at the point of going to France to study art, you can imagine how much she was thrilled in anticipation by her surroundings. The woman art-student in France in my time was a rarity, and though it was several years later that my wife went there, her experiences, before the days of female emancipation, were so curious that I am always urging her to write them.

So I imagine that May Alcott's letters of her pioneer experiences would be most interesting, and I trust you will draw upon them largely. I repeat that I am most sorry to be like a ship that passes in the night, without hailing, but in the effort to be helpful, I can only think of Isobel Osbourne, who was a young girl at Grez during her mother's stay there in 1876–7, and might have some knowledge of May Alcott. There were, by the way, two Inns at Grez, Chevillon's, where we, the Stevensons and our band stayed, and the other, whose name I forget, and which I fancy was considered the most respectable, though that may be because it was slightly more expensive. Coming from Concord, whose philosophy would I am sure have been tried by the general disorder at Chevillon's, Miss Alcott may have preferred the second of these places. It is hard trailing witches of so transitory a thing as our life in France, though it is a part of my religion to believe it was a good life. I am certain that the unfortunate and sophisticated youth of today will never see the like of it. I am

Sincerely yours,

WILL H. LOW.

And in pursuance of Mr. Low's suggestion, a letter went to Isobel Osbourne, now Mrs. Salisbury Field, who graciously responded, recalling some of her memories of the year '77.

She wrote that as a girl in her early teens, she well remembered May Alcott, who formed a friendship with her mother, before her marriage to Stevenson, at which time they were often together at Julien's studio. In this connection she says:

I distinctly remember meeting her at Julien's studio, in the old Passage des Panoramas, off the Boulevard des Italiens. I was very young then and of course had read and adored "Little Women", and I was thrilled when told that the tall, distinguished-looking lady, who wore her hair in curls, was "Amy" of that beloved family. I gazed at her with awe and admiration, just a little disenchanted to find her grown-up and reserved. I know I asked her several questions diffidently, and she answered kindly, but in a bored manner as though she had heard them very often before, "Yes, Laurie was a real person." "No, she did not marry him," that sort of thing.

As I remember her through such a mist of years, she was tall, very slender and graceful, and wore her hair in long curls down her back, a rather

unusual fashion even for those days. I was much
interested in her, but she naturally was not particularly interested in a young person of fourteen,
who stared at her with absorbed attention and asked
all the usual questions. As I said, we left Grez before
1879, but she knew my mother at Julien's studio,
for I often saw them there talking together.

Yours truly,

Isobel Field.

Serena, Carpinteria, California,
July 24, 1926.

These slender links that bind May Alcott to
the little group that was to create in America
an era of art are well worthy of preservation, for
she shared in the dream that all the others of
that group determined "should come true." She
was not destined to aid it as extensively as many,
but from the first her heart was with them, and
by her influence more than by her creative work
she helped to bring about results for which we
should be truly grateful. The Concord Art Center,
which she established; the lump of clay that she
gave to Daniel Chester French; the classes that she
taught; her little book, instructing young art students regarding life and opportunities abroad; and
lastly her own excellent productions which, had she
lived, might have fulfilled those high hopes cherished

[225]

by her family, and by herself — all have contributed to our national heritage in the art world.

In that summer of 1877, when this notable group of American art students were summering at Grez, some had already returned to New York, with great ambitions and small means, and of these "home comers", as they were called, a little coterie decided to make some special effort towards the realization of their purpose. On a June evening, four young artists met at 103 East Fifteenth Street, in what had once been a carriage house but which had been transformed into a charming dwelling for a young couple whose literary and artistic qualities were to count much in the life of their generation, — Mr. and Mrs. Richard Watson Gilder. The four were Augustus Saint-Gaudens, Wyatt Eaton, Walter Shirlaw, and Helena de Kay Gilder, and when the meeting had been called to order, Saint-Gaudens made the motion: "*Resolved*, That an association be formed by those present with the object of advancing the interests of art in America: the same to be entitled 'The American Art Association'."

The new association continued to grow and flourish and its first exhibition was held a few months later. It was at the beginning regarded as quite unimportant and revolutionary in character, but soon its value in the art world made itself felt and its more staid competitor, the National Academy of Design, from time to time admitted the younger painters to its ranks. And finally, in after years, the two opposing associations were merged in one.

At the time of its birth, the new society was hailed by a few of the older men as the advent of a new day. Among these was George Fuller, who had long struggled against an unappreciative public and had been driven to give up art for farming, but in the end had returned to his first love and to a brighter day. He was among the society's enthusiasts, as was another unappreciated painter, Homer Martin, who struggled to the end without public recognition. In those days Whistler was wholly without honor in his own country, and it was one of the first tasks of the young society to dispatch a member to Baltimore, where a picture by Whistler was procured, probably the first of his to be exhibited in this country; and in 1882 his masterpiece, the portrait of his Mother, now in the Luxembourg, was first shown in New York at the Society's exhibition of that year.

In these beginnings May Alcott played her little part, nor will she be forgotten by her fellow associates, though they outstripped her in the race.

CHAPTER X

The Passing of Marmee

THE coming of May's portrait was an event to
which her mother looked forward with keen expectation, it being the next best thing to the return
of the original. And in May, 1877, she chronicles
in her journal the fact that it is on its way to
Concord. She also notes the loss of one of Concord's leading citizens:

"We are daily expecting Miss Peckham's portrait of May, which Geo. Lombard kindly took
charge of and forwarded per steamer for Boston.
Mr. William Munroe is to be buried tomorrow, a
good man and a great loss to the town of Concord,
as he was generous towards Art and the best culture
of the young people, was always a patron of May
and helped to promote her efforts to establish a
free studio for the benefit of those who could not
pay for the use of good studios in the fine arts.
He built at his own expense the Library which
cost $75,000, the building alone, and contributed
valuable pictures, drawings, maps, books and busts.

"Nice letters from May; as the hot weather
comes on she proposes going to 'Grez', a pretty,

primitive suburban town where she can be free to sketch, and live cheaply and coolly; she is very well now, but the hot season may not be so good for her in those close quarters, although a constant flowing fountain keeps the air pure."

Mrs. Alcott's next entry tells of the arrival of the portrait, which gives her much satisfaction, although she regrets that May's hat smacks of Paris rather than of Concord:

"May 12, 1877, *Miss Peckham's Picture*. Great day for the Alcotts. Picture arrived from Paris, the hot-bed of High Art, forwarded by Mr. Geo. Lombard from Liverpool. Miss Peckham has caught May's air and pose most successfully, and her 'suaviter in mode' of tone; — years ago when her eyes were bright, and her heart was light, and she thought of Love and glory. The tone of high coloring is more the fashion than it has been, everything is more intense; Life itself is short and swift, music is loud and strong, more sound than harmony. The picture is May and nobody else, but the hat is Madame Williams' 'Salon Chapeau.' May's own pretty hair, with her blue velvet snood, would have suited my taste better but Paris is all crimson and gilt, nude or dressed for exhibition."

A fortnight later Mrs. Alcott continues her record of home doings:

"June 1st. Confer about the Thoreau house. Sent off letter by *Marathon*. Mr. Cook dines here. Louisa goes to Boston. June 5th, letter from May. I read with intense interest 'Daniel Deronda', it was tedious as a serial, but the plot is worked up with the finest intellectual machinery, the author's subtle wit and moral perception is quite remarkable. Hayes and Wheeler, after a long conflict with the Democrats, elected President, and Vice-President of the United States. The local government of the South are in fearful anarchy, and the financial affairs of the country in a general state of depression; a new impulse will be given, it is to be hoped, to trade, manufacturers and internal improvements, under the more honest and prudential government. The last year created fearful factions throughout the country, and the fraudulent rings have led to distrust and dishonesty.

"There are persons whose fate it is, in writing their Biographies, to announce their own strength and weakness more distinctly than any one else has done, and draw a clear distinctive line about their own reputation; such is the case with Miss Martineau, whose book I am reading with great interest. When we consider her great mental gifts, her long labors, her service to the good causes of her day, her freedom from all cant, her courage, her cheerfulness and her loyalty to her friends, she must be pronounced one of the most eminent and useful persons of her time."

A number of brief extracts follow, touching upon home matters and old-time memories:

"July 14th. Letters from May. Anna preparing for her new house, the Thoreau house, will begin moving on Monday. Another change in our domestic arrangements. I am persuaded our health will be better for the change, and it will be better for the boys, nearer their companions, and the social requirements will be of advantage to them."

"July 15th. My health is good but I am at times feeble, generally weaker. We have two good women now to do the work. This I hope will prove a relief to Louisa, whose cares were too many; and her various responsibilities are unfavorable to her nervous system."

"27th – 28th. I have been reading the Life of George Cabot. My father was secretary of the 'Marine Ins. Office' for 40 years, 20 of which Mr. Cabot was the President. My father felt the greatest respect for his judgment and opinion on all subjects maritime, commercial, or political; I have always wondered that no Biography of Mr. Cabot has been written. He was President of the Hartford Convention, convened in 1814, to take measures for the relief of the New England States, and to combine in resisting any plan for disunion of the states, which the radicals, or 'hot-heads', as Mr. Cabot used to call them, might be desiring. The exhaustive embargo, the War of 1812 for 'Free trade and Sailors' rights', the annexation of Louisiana by purchase of the French, everything disorganizing occurred to our commercial affairs, and our factions. Mr. Cabot's commercial and financial knowledge would have made him a fit finance minister for any empire. He died in 1823, 80 years of age.'

"Letter from May containing these leaves from the Studio", notes Mrs. Alcott, and at the head of this page in her journal, two pressed leaves are carefully pasted beside the words, "May's studio, Paris, July 27, 1877", with the comment:

"She continues at the school where from the models she catches fine forms and features and improves all occasions to perfect herself in the anatomy of the human body that her drawing may be faultless, before the coloring finishes up the lights and shades, the pose, and tone of this wonderful conception of creative Wisdom that the highest Art alone can imitate with anything like success. Her return is still in the far distance of time, but if we are all well, and get these fine letters from week to week, why should we not be content; Life is much the thing we make it, by cheerful endurance of its evils and acceptance of joys, or the anxious forebodings of discontent and ennui."

"August 11, 1877. A letter from May; thinks much of going to 'Couture', who seems now to be the finishing up of all the artists. She seems to know her needs, and how to meet them. I have much confidence in her plans for getting her artistic help. The Miss Peckhams are on their way to Switzerland, and Alice Wheeler goes to Germany to meet her brother this leaves May alone. The artist friend, Miss Cassatt, will be her companion for the present; she thinks of going to Versailles, and Trianon, on a pleasant excursion, and to the Theatre Française; these little trips will do her good, break up the loneliness of her apartment."

After considering the plan to study under Couture, May finally decided that this painter's

pupils were not receiving sufficient attention, although they were paying a high price to this
master, who was too absorbed in his own work to
give them more than a casual criticism. About
this time she writes of attending an interesting
exhibition:

"We went yesterday to see the ten great pictures competing for the 'Prix de Rome', which
allows a French painter of sufficient merit, three
or four years in Rome for study at the expense of
the government. Tomorrow, the judges decide the
question and everyone is greatly excited on the
subject as so many students have been at work
for ten or fifteen years in hopes to get it. Krug
was one of five hundred who made the sketches,
and was one of the 24 chosen (some years ago) to
paint a picture from his sketch, but as they have
to be shut up with their models, and no inter-
course with the world in general allowed, and no
change from the original sketch, he found it too
difficult and gave it up. The ten we saw were
very interesting, the subject given them was, the
Gauls entering Rome and tweaking the old gray-
headed Roman by the hair, who resents the in-
sult, and strikes the Gaul, which was the general
signal for massacre. It was a fine subject, and in

two of them was superbly treated, for the color was rich, the composition strong and the drawing fine. We wandered around the crowded rooms and then crossing the bridge, the river being gay with boats and the view lovely, we took a look at the Louvre treasures and then I walked home. . . . This afternoon we three went to Blashfield's studio, and had a nice time rummaging among his fine tapestries, brocades, fine costumes and much bric-à-brac, he has collected a great many things and has excellent taste. A fine carved kind of sofa, which opens and makes a chest, he has just had made for Abby Manning, with old panels and superb great griffins for arms. It's exceedingly handsome and will make Boston people envious who see it. I should like to get enough things for a studio, but I must wait till after I have done my great picture and then I can indulge in these nice things which are so dear to an artist's heart."

The return from Europe of Miss Bartol, bringing May's Salon picture as well as the latest news from the young painter, was a special delight to Mrs. Alcott, who wrote in her journal:

"Miss Lizzie Bartol arrives in the *Parthia*, brings May's picture, still-life group. We shall have it soon. Miss Bartol saw May, she says in a note, and 'found her the same hearty soul as ever', pleasant tribute to my good child."

"August 22nd. I write to Geo. B. Emerson in the same familiar and affectionate manner his letter was written. Federal Court memories are the tender tie which unites us at this late hour of our lives, being 60 years since dear Louisa and S. J. May made sweet music for us in the beloved presence of my mother and father, and Eliza filled our house with glee, when we all joined in the chorus of the 'Woodland Hollow,' or 'Auld Lang Syne,' or 'Home, Sweet Home.' It is delightful at this distant period to be met by one who has so fondly cherished these dear kindred, and home of my girlhood. He regularly dined with us on Saturdays, and the summer of 1817 he graduated from Harvard in the same class with my brother. Mr. Emerson was too sick to return to his home at Kennebunk, Maine, and my mother had him brought to Federal Court where he remained very sick for 5 weeks." [Here the paragraph abruptly ends and the entries which followed have evidently been lost or destroyed.]

"Sept. 1st, 1877. The year nearly closed over May's absence. My health has been unusually good. I have missed her at times very much but each day has brought its occupations and I am here to gratefully record the good progress of her Art, and the good health of the family.

"We have had a pleasant call from Miss Putnam the associate of Miss Holley at Lattsburg, the colored school. She reaffirms what Miss Holley has often stated of the great utility of the school. The poor Whites beg the permission to come and be taught, for even a little culture makes everything so much more respectable for the emancipated blacks that they feel the distinction of races much lessened. Miss P. has introduced much of the kindergarten plans, and they succeed remarkably with it. Action and industry are new to them. They are soon made to feel the benefits of order and method. They are taught everything from gardening to sewing and reading."

May's letters continued to bring her mother much entertainment, and on September 2d she describes a jolly evening spent with her friend Miss Cassatt and the Misses Stearns. The latter having entertained the party by driving to a restaurant in the "Bois", for ices:

"We started, it then being after ten o'clock, but the city never seems to sleep, all the world being abroad apparently till morning. The avenues lined with big trees and pretty shrubs looked like enchantment. When away from the brilliant street lights and after going a long way winding up and down, we turned into a great court-yard filled with little tables surrounded by a set of nice looking people sipping their coffee, wine or absynthe. The dense darkness of the wood surrounding it being illuminated by colored lamps giving the whole thing a most theatrical appearance. Waiters appeared from all directions and our carriages drove off into the darkness while we descended to partake of our ices and cake, which at this late hour proved a little too cooling. The café itself was a great building in imitation of a chalet with balconies and colored tiles fine to see, and we felt as if in a play, all was so fantastic. Afterwards we drove home in the soft air leaving the Stearnses at their door after telling them what a nice lark we considered it."

She concludes this letter with the words:

"Thiers died this morning at 6 o'clock, at Saint-Germain, so the coming election is more to be dreaded than ever, as he had great influence in keeping things peaceful. Perhaps it's as well to flee Paris before matters look blacker than at present."

THE PASSING OF MARMEE
Her description of Thiers' funeral follows:

"The funeral of Thiers has been the sensation of the hour, and all the city has turned out to do him honor, tho' Madame Thiers did not agree to the Government doing it all as they wanted to, and so put it through according to his last wishes and at her own expense, of which I approve.

"Rose and Kate went to see the grand procession but no one was admitted to Père la Chaise without a pass, so they stood in the mud and rain for hours, and saw only the hearse loaded with bright flowers and the silver cords held by distinguished friends and followed by his three carriages wound up in crepe, quite empty, with only the lacqueys hanging on behind. Then troops, and the artists and great societies, and members of the institute, then more carriages, and an immense crowd on foot with yellow immortels in their button-holes. They feared some outbreak, but all passed off serenely tho' the Republicans have lost their best friend."

The final pages of Marmee's journal bear but a few lines penned smoothly and legibly but very faintly, as if there were little strength remaining in the writer's ever-industrious fingers. But her thought is still centering on her artist child:

"Our last letters from May announce her arrival in England; she hopes to spend 6 months or a year in studying water-colors. She seems in good heart and hope about her plans for the future."

In her letters written towards the close of the summer, May had outlined her decision to continue her work in London, where the opportunities to sell her pictures were so much better than in France.

In the meantime, the communications from Concord told of the plan to close Orchard House, and to make the Thoreau House, which had been recently purchased, the family headquarters. After the death of Sophia Thoreau, the house where Henry Thoreau had died in 1862 had been secured by Mrs. Pratt, for herself and children. Louisa was anxious that they should have a comfortable home, and after Mrs. Pratt had invested what she could in the purchase, Louisa paid the remainder, noting in her journal in April, 1877:

"Helped to buy the house for Nan. So she has her wish and is happy. When shall I have mine? Ought to be contented with knowing I help both sisters with my brains. But I'm selfish, and want to go away and rest in Europe. Never shall."

May's artist friend Miss Austin, who was returning to America early in the autumn, had under-
taken to carry out a plan to paint the portraits of
both Mr. and Mrs. Alcott, and this suggestion
was eagerly discussed in May's home letters at this
period, as she felt that the family possessed no
satisfactory likenesses of their gifted parents to
hand down to posterity. She also suggested that a
little later a portrait must be done of Louisa.

The failure to carry out this plan, owing to
Mrs. Alcott's failing health, was a great disappointment to the artist of the family, who had penned
most minute instructions regarding the preparation of her parents for their sittings, writing in
this connection:

"See that both dress with greatest care and
don't let father spat his hair flat, but let it fluff
out, which makes it look thick and silvery and is
more becoming to his long face than if brushed or
wet a little, which is dreadful. Now mind and
stand over him so he shan't wet or flatten it!
Mother must study which is her most becoming
cap. The embroidery of the cap will look well in
the picture. While father is being painted see that
he wears his clean broadcloth all the time. If
she prefers to do father on a large scale at his

writing-table, let her do it, as we have no striking
picture of him, the crayon being too soft, and not
at all what an immortal picture of him should be,
and it will look fine at the Library opposite Emerson, or alongside, to be numbered among Concord
lights. One of the pointed antique chairs tho'
uncomfortable to sit in, may look well in Austin's
picture."

As has been stated, this plan was never carried
out, and May's own portrait remained the one from
which her family derived the keenest satisfaction.
Of its position in his study, her father wrote:

"Artists have fine tastes and you shall see
whether we have honored these in hanging your
picture. Anna's removal takes sundry things or-
namental and useful from the rooms, above and
below. The boys' book-case from my study with
the rest, so my book-case takes its place, and your
picture with Turner's portrait over it, hangs there
on the wall instead, and the apostles beside it.
The table that stood under the west window now
stands with flowers under your picture. The light
falls from the south windows and brings out your
best expression as we stand at the entry door.
And my study table now faces the fair young
lady as I write, not a single disparaging criticism

as yet from the many, but approving from all. We are all delighted at having found its place, after many trials and discussions."

While the process of moving was under way in Concord, May was writing cheerfully from London, following the home doings and hoping that the change to the new house would be beneficial to her mother, to whom she wrote on October 8, heading the sheet with the words: "Happy Birthday", and noting her disappointment that her mother had not been well enough to sit for her portrait:

MY DEAREST MARMEE, — I am so glad to see your handwriting again as it seems a long while since you wrote me one of your good letters and Lu has made excuses the last week or two for your not adding a word to the envelope which I get so regularly. I hope by this time you are settled at Annie's for the winter, where you will have the amusement of people looking in upon you occasionally and some little passing in the street to vary the scene from Wheeler crossing to the barn, and Moore's cows going home at night. I am sorry you were not well enough to sit for your portrait but as it all happened to turn out for Austin and Lu, it's better as it is. I had a nice letter from her yesterday saying it had all been postponed and thanking me for thinking of it at all. [May touches upon the various little gifts she is sending home and then describes her life at the new boarding place in London, and her recreation trips with friends:]

There is always something pleasant going on of an evening, and then Warner drops in and takes me for a spree as he did yesterday, coming at luncheon and doing some bric-à-brac shops together, the Temple Church, Inner Temple, and all those pretty squares given over to lawyers and barristers who have their apartments there and the courts not far off. The library for them is like an embattled fortress with its antique tower, its wide marble bridge over a kind of moat, and colored windows which I took as a sure sign of its being a church. All this in the heart of London within a stone's throw of Fleet Street. [May closes with the words:]

I imagine you all celebrating Marmee's birthday today, and I wish I had something to send more than this lace, which is real edging, as Marmee will see it will be pretty for the neck of her best dress, or somewhere.

Bless you all round, my dear family, and write me about Marmee, for Lu only knows how far

London and Concord are when one is sick. It takes so long to hear from you. Marmee must n't be sick again till I can come and tend her, for I seem to be the only strong one just now and I hope I may keep so. Good bye, dear Marmee, from your May.

During the next few weeks Mrs. Alcott failed rapidly, and her final communication to the child whom she felt she would not see again, was but a brief farewell. In answer May wrote in great anxiety but without a full realization of her mother's grave condition:

My dear Marmee, — Your little note nearly broke my heart, not to be there with my arms round your neck when you are so ill, and your baby, if no other daughter, should be with you. I paint away and try not to get anxious but hope for the best, and take this minute before the mail closes to tell you the great news about my Dudley picture, for I know it will please you as much as the Salon success did. To begin, yesterday I asked Miss Warner to lunch with me and go to the Dudley. So we went as agreed upon and of course looked about for the owl-panel, which to our surprise we found in a corner, badly hung but with a great star on the frame showing it was already *sold*, and that at the *private view* where only invited guests were present. Was n't that a triumph, and for $50. which was thought very little for it, but as it took me only one morning to paint it I considered it enough, don't you? Only a few other pictures were decorated with stars, so I felt particularly proud and know you will for me. The exhibition is exceedingly good even compared with Paris Art, and I was surprised that without favor, the owl should ever have been accepted, much less sold.

These light-hearted descriptions of her artistic successes, which May hoped would cheer and entertain her mother, found her so ill that all hope of her rallying was given up, and when, on November 18, it was certain that she could not be much longer with them, Mr. Alcott wrote to May that even if she should sail at once she would not be likely to find her mother still alive, upon arrival, and he added:

"The dear patient is patience itself, every virtue that shone during her active life, now burns the more brightly during her weakness. Not many daughters have been blessed with a mother so unselfish and so noble. I shall hardly enjoy the old house again after her departure."

THE PASSING OF MARMEE

Although failing rapidly, Mrs. Alcott was moved to her daughter Anna's new home, where she breathed her last in less than a fortnight.

Only two more brief entries remain in the precious journal which so constantly records the writer's keen interest in others and her self-forgetfulness. There are no complaints of failing health, no querulous repinings, no self-pity, or demands that the idolized youngest daughter shall return to brighten her last days. Up to the very end she displays her vital interest in the welfare of her country, and of its less fortunate citizens, both black and white, as well as of the latest doings in the world of art and literature, and her keen gift of literary discernment and nicely balanced appreciation of the best reveal the dominant power of mind and spirit surmounting all mere ills of the flesh.

Just at the end, she touches upon her serious physical condition, and on the next to the last page of her journal she writes very faintly:

"I am quite irregular about my journal, but my health is so uncertain. Dyspepsia and constantly increasing difficulties of the heart and chest. I have a nurse as I require so much done through the night."

And then follows the closing entry, penned on her seventy-seventh birthday, when she refrains from any mention of her illness and characteristically records only her gratitude for all her blessings:

"Oct. 8th: The day has been most mercifully extended to me and beautifully celebrated even to the coming of May's letter full of pleasant news."

These four lines stand at the head of an otherwise blank leaf and affixed to the page opposite is the writer's pen, just as she laid it down. Beneath it in the handwriting of her daughter, Louisa, are the words:

"Marmee's pen, left in the book when she had written the last lines, on her 77th birthday, Oct. 8, 1877, at the old home."

So ends the journal of that last year of Mrs. Alcott's life, dedicated to May, and beneath the handle of the pen is tucked Louisa's loving and grieving message to this sister so far away, written November 25, in pencil. In this sorrowful note, she writes that Marmee is at rest, after two months of pain and weariness. That she sleeps sweetly and peacefully and that her last words and smiles were a benediction to them all. The day before she passed, she pointed to May's picture and said smiling, "Little May", and almost at the end she murmured, "A smile is as good as a prayer."

The sad message, with a tiny lock of Marmee's hair attached to it, reached the heart-broken daughter so far from home, who at the first reproached herself most bitterly for having given to her art this last year that she might have spent in ministering to her mother. But after those first days of overwhelming grief, May faced the situation bravely, determining to work with a redoubled vigor to the end that her mother's faith in her should not be proved in vain.

After receiving the home letters which told her of the services held for her mother, May writes that she is very sad and lonely although her friends are showing her every possible kindness.

"These days are very dark just now and I wander about among the pictures and sit listening to the music in Westminster Abbey, and so get through them, and avoid the people constantly coming both with messages and flowers to express their sympathy. For I cannot speak of Marmee, or control my tears enough to try to see any one yet, and a boarding-house is an excellent place to avoid people, I find, and one can be as much alone as is possible.

"Your letter of Nov. 29, I have just read and I am much cheered by it, for all seemed so beautiful, particularly the saying good-bye to Marmee at twilight and only yourselves. That suited me and I was with you in spirit I know, as I feel sure, *she has come to me*, as I did not go to her. I try to do as she would have me and perhaps shall work the better for the real suffering I never knew till now. I get through the days by painting busily, but at night it is hard not to have a good cry, though I look out at a bright star that twinkles in at my window and feel it is Marmee smiling at me, and so I say a little prayer from my heart and go to sleep."

CHAPTER XI

Clouds and Sunshine

THE year 1878, which was to bring into May
Alcott's life the romance she had dreamed of,
but never thought to realize, dawned gloomily.
Never had she experienced so sad a New Year's
day as that spent in the lonely boarding house in
England, so far away from all those dear to her,
with whom she longed to share her grief, and shut
in by dense London fogs, which settled down upon
the city so thickly as to make it impossible for
her even to carry on her work.

December had been a month of gloom and
sadness, despite the kindly sympathy of many
London friends. In reply to the letters which
brought the details of her mother's passing with
all the precious memories of her last hours on
earth, May wrote remorsefully that she could not
forgive herself for not returning home, when she
first knew that there was little hope of her mother's
recovery:

If I *had only sailed* in October, or even in time
for one look from her dear eyes, it would have
comforted me, for it seems now when too late, that

all the Art honors Europe can offer me, will never take the place of feeling once more her arms round my neck and her soft cheek against mine. . . .

My only comfort is that perhaps my letters and little triumphs here have given her more pleasure than if I had staid at home with her, for I was n't the kind thoughtful daughter that Annie has been to her, and I have so much to reproach myself with that it seems as if I can never forgive myself.

Now dear father, write me a sweet comforting letter and think of me kindly though I did n't come to help and comfort as I should have, could I have realized what it is to lose one's mother and be thousands of miles away.

Will Lu write a little sketch of her or perhaps make a memoir from her doings so full of philanthropy and events interesting to all, not merely her personal friends who knew and loved her, but those who must admire the heroism of the woman's life and her connection with interesting facts and people?

Good-bye dear family my head aches with crying and I can see no longer this bright Sunday overhead but so dark to me in my little lonely room, up three flights.

Yours

MAY

P. S. My little friend of 5 years, Harry Hammond, comes softly in and pats my cheek saying, "Don't cry, my dear May," then cuddles down by my side and puts his round cheek to mine for some kisses. I call him my little comforter and try to tell him stories.

Again she notes the kindness of those about her:

"Everyone is so kind to me here that hard as it is not to be with you, it has shown me the kind side of strangers that I should never have suspected, and the real sympathy expressed by people I have hardly spoken to, is certainly better than none. If I can only get through a day or two courageously perhaps it will be possible to paint a little and so throw off this death at my heart."

May finds it hard not to reproach herself for leaving home while Marmee was in failing health, but realizes that she made the decision herself, and must now bear her regrets as bravely as possible, though the many reminders of her mother make this most difficult. She writes:

"I have looked over all her letters to me and arranged them through my tears according to their dates, the biggest interval being from Sept. 19, to the dear little note bidding me farewell, of Nov. 11th. I shall look at the figure, in the big arm chair, with the white cap sitting in father's study, a little photograph of which I brought with me, as my shrine and wonder how I could ever have left it."

The dense London fogs add much to the general depression and May describes the days which are too dark even for carrying on her work:

"On waking this morning to find the thickest of London fogs settled over everything, I gave up my working on the Spanish Girl with Miss Hughes as I promised to do, and stayed at home, with the gas lighted everywhere, until one of the gentlemen brought a great jar of preserved prunes to amuse us while waiting for light to come again outside. It was the darkest fog I have ever seen and quite suited my state of mind for I was thinking of that Saturday just four weeks ago when your sad letters reached me and I knew for the first time that Marmee had passed away. Every Sunday I allow the five hours earlier for your time on that side of the Atlantic, and have a little tender weep for Marmee at half past seven in my little room when I feel so near her.

But oh for the touch of a vanished hand,
And the sound of a voice that is still.

[254]

CLOUDS AND SUNSHINE

"Her last little note, every word of which is on my lips and in my thoughts all the time, would have taken me home but I felt that it was then too late, as it proved, for I was sure it must be the great final farewell, and I never knew before how dearly I loved her and how tender was the tie between us. I always think how precious were those days when we went driving round Concord together in the early mornings, and picture her seated on the rustic bench afterward taking her cup of tea, looking so sweet and handsome in her little crepe bonnet."

She praises her sister Louisa for her unselfish devotion to all the family.

"I can picture Father in his gray dressing gown and foresee a happy old age for him spent with his pet daughter in that snug little home without care or responsibility. Certainly, dear Lu, you can never be grateful enough that *you* have been the one who could make dear Marmee, and Papa too, so comfortable and happy these last years by your generosity and devotion, for money has done what affection alone could never do, unromantic as it sounds to say so, and you have delighted in making us all happy in our own way tho' much of your own life and health has been sacrificed in doing it, and this I feel more perhaps than anybody.

"Perhaps Lu will come and spend next summer with me to refresh her mind and body if she is strong enough after the next few months of rest and quiet. Please tell me all the plans that are under consideration and I feel sure you will decide to sell Apple Slump, as I shall never want to live there again, or waste my strength, or have Lu do it in keeping such an establishment running. If father's eyes are giving him trouble he could n't enjoy his old study much and a little cozy winter library, like that at Nan's, would answer, I should think, and would be a protection to Annie also. How does Papa feel about it? If I can only get over this present grief and regret I think I can go on with my work and gain more triumphs for Marmee to enjoy, for I am sure she is always near me and interested in what interests me as much as father and sisters can be. . . . I shall try to do all and be all that she would have me, and if I fail I shall at least have had the satisfaction of knowing that I have tried faithfully to please her and follow the advice of a little verse she once pasted in my desk and which I think you will find there even now.

> Be good, sweet maid, and let who will be clever;
> Do noble things, not dream them, all day long:
> And so make life, death, and that last forever
> One grand sweet song.
>
> KINGSLEY.

"So dear girls don't you think it best for me to stay and *do* great things having dreamed of them for so many years? I know you will advise me and help me, and if mine can't be a happy domestic life, such as I have longed and prayed for, perhaps the good God meant me for great things in other ways. Lu got her success through much trouble and pain and perhaps this sacrifice I have freely chosen to make in losing one year of Marmee's life, may make me work the better."

A month later, she is steadily going on with her work, and is sending home lively communications to cheer her sisters. In the letter which follows describing her London quarters, she mentions the young Swiss, who was so soon to play a large part in her life:

My Dearest Dears, — I begin my first letter from my new little bower which is as cozy as you can possibly imagine for my little duds, new Delft vases, etc. when scattered round with an eye for effect make quite an ensemble and very attractive snuggery. The Pierces run in and out and also the Warners, Hughes and my nice Swiss, who comes to play chess and read to me evenings when I can't use my eyes. My little parlor is so small it can't help but be cozy, with a round table in one corner at which I am now writing, a rack and picture, ink-stand, portfolio and antique dagger in full display. A little couch on one side with big picture and panels over it, and a long table with three pictures on it. . . . In the one window which has long green curtains and close shades, is a low mahogany what-not fitted in as a sort of window-seat, only higher, which makes a nice closet with close doors, and on top stands my monk and panels, my brass brazier, owl, and my two Delft vases which are thoroughly handsome and admired by everyone. The large one, I throw cards and photographs into, Lu's sitting one, standing in front of the brazier, while one of mother and father are on my table as I write. On the whole, with my two big arm-chairs, my little room impresses everyone as the picture of comfort and taste.

Last night as I sat after eating a hot muffin toasted before my blazing fire, held there stuck onto my gilded dagger for a fork, and washed down by a cup of nice cocoa, I was surprised by the Pierces, Hughes and my Swiss, — all coming at once, which so appalled me that I told them they would have to sit down in one another's laps as the room was so very small, Mr. Pierce saying that he chose me to sit in his; they brought me the *St. Nicholas*, to read Lu's story, also the *Nation*, and were nice and kind, inviting me to dine on Sunday (today).

Certainly there is much more comfort to be had here, only perhaps I should n't have moved so soon if I had n't thought Lu would be coming along very soon to make it social and nice. At any rate, I shall do a lot of pot-boilers here and have a fling at the exhibitions and then go to Paris again for hard study, which I never should have left if I could have foreseen events. . . . The boarders mourn my absence at 26 and the two devoted bachelors expressed real regret at my leaving, but I did not ask them to come and see me, though they had been so kind. . . . The still-life I take to the Ladies exhibition tomorrow, is much better than the Salon one, though the same strong style.

A few weeks later she writes of exhibiting her work:

March 3rd, 1878.

I have another success to announce in having two pictures accepted and well hung, at the Ladies Exhibition, which is a small collection but patronized by the Marchioness of Lorne, Lady this and Lady that, and all quite fine. Miss Gatts and Miss Hughes were both refused, so I am alone in

[259]

my glory, as at the Salon, having simply sent the
pictures in for the jury to judge of, and then left
them to their fate, which always so far has been a
happy one. So it's lucky May, I hope, to the end
of the chapter. What I sent was a very large still-
life twice the size of the Salon one you have, of
books, the little green lamp, and my precious owl
standing atop of the manuscripts, the loose white
leaves of which is about the best piece of painting
I ever did. You will remember my describing it
to you when I did it alone in Paris during the hot
weather, and Krug saw and praised it, particularly
the book.

Her next communication brings an unexpected
surprise to those at home, for on March 11, 1878,
she wrote announcing her engagement to the young
Swiss, Ernest Nieriker, whom she had frequently
referred to in her letters and who had been a fellow
boarder with her during the weeks of sorrow following her mother's death. He had proved a sympathetic and devoted friend. They were thoroughly
congenial in their tastes, and though he was a
business man with a very modest income, and
considerably her junior, he was also a fine musician,
who sympathized with her artistic aspirations, and
charmed her by the strains of his violin. She wrote

that if she married him, after a short engagement, she should not relinquish her art, but would continue her work with added effort and inspiration.

This announcement, which was no doubt something of a shock to those at home, was followed on March 24th by still more startling news, that of May's marriage, which is best described in her own words:

"The last week has been one of such hurry and excitement that I hardly know where to begin to tell you how and what has happened, for I hardly realize it all myself except that the serene contentment and quiet happiness that have entirely taken possession of me keep the fact that some great event has taken place constantly before me. I will try and give you a connected account of it all, and if I am a little more incoherent than usual you may lay it to my ecstatic state of mind just now.

"Sunday evening, Ernest came and said he had letters of business calling him to the Continent and he must decide at once which offer to accept. If that in France, or in Russia, we must separate possibly for a year. This is what I had dreaded and I said so, but as he felt as badly if not worse than I did, I made the best of it and we laid our plans with the prospect of being together later. So I still kept silent to my London friends feeling that I wanted to keep him to myself for these last few days, and made various excuses to all and waited. On Monday, Ernest came in saying, 'May, I cannot be happy to part. Why should we not have this year together? Life seems too short to lose so much. If you will consent to forego a fine wedding and fine trousseau and begin with me now, we can enjoy so much together.'

"Well, dear papa, and girls, you know how I have longed for love, and just such a life. It did not need much urging and I said, 'Yes, I will go and it is the wisest and happiest thing we can do.'

"I at once made my few preparations. My wedding-dress was of brown silken stuff with pretty plumed hat to match gloves and all in harmony. My simple affairs were soon in order.

"On Friday, I drove with a friend to the office of the Register, at which place Ernest met me with the necessary papers, and officers, and we were married. A heavy gold ring put on with a loving kiss finishing the ceremony.

"We then drove to Waterloo Station, catching the train for Southampton, where we were to take the boat for Havre.

"Friday was a lovelier morning than London

often sees and a happier couple than ourselves as we rode through the pretty green country to the sea could not have been found in all the world.

"We had a most delightful passage and arrived at Havre on a fine morning, the harbor lovely in the early light. . . . We strolled around the picturesque place looking for a pretty apartment in which to rest like real French people for a week, while Ernest is deciding upon his Paris offer. Leaving our luggage at the Customs we trotted along, going in to look wherever upon a door appeared, 'Chambre à louer.' At last we found this cozy crimson suite, with its clock and vases, like all French apartments, its canopied bed, its sofas and curtains, the long windows looking out on a sunny street with a pretty stone vine-covered house just opposite, and nice smiling landlady to oversee everything.

"So we here begin our honeymoon ménage and I have already given it a home look with our own little things scattered about and a bright open-fire burning.

"Last evening, Anna's heart would have danced a jig of joy to have seen us sitting there so happily talking over our wedding adventures. Then Ernest took his violin and played his lovely German melodies. . . . We mean to live our own life free

[263]

from conventionalities. Indeed this foreign way seems to me ideal, more so than anything I ever hoped could fall to my lot by any possibility, lucky as I am in most things. I shall have long days for painting.

"I have never dreamed of such serene happiness as I have known since Friday, when as man and wife Ernest and I left Southampton. My future seems so full of beauty and of joy I can think of nothing else. The lonely artistic life that once satisfied me seems the most dreary in the world. Our tastes are so congenial it seems impossible that we shall ever clash, and even were it otherwise I find myself for the first time quite willing to bend to a stronger will and wiser head than my own. Ernest is so gentle yet so firm, and I know he loves me so tenderly that I yield easily, so you see how changed is your wilful, strong-minded sister. She is as gentle and sweet, dear Nanny, as yourself."

A month later, May writes from Meudon, where they have been able to secure satisfactory quarters, not far from Paris. She expresses the hope that they are settled for at least a year in this new home.

"Ernest has accepted a fine position in a great mercantile house in Paris, where as Inspector

General he will have an ample salary, and where his former experience in Geneva will be of great service. They seem delighted to have secured him and gave him a week to prepare before entering on his duties."

After describing their search for a desirable abiding place, she tells of their selection of Meudon, which is but fifteen minutes from Paris by rail, and of their finding what they wanted almost immediately upon arrival there, in search of a home. She writes:

"The house stood in the midst of a superb garden filled with blossoming shrubs, trees and flowers behind, and in front was a neat yard with borders of flowers. A glass portico admitted us, and we found a very old French lady to show us about. Our rooms are on the right, and consist of a salon, dining-room, kitchen, two chambers with closets, bath-room, etc., a pretty flight of ivy-covered steps leading into the garden behind.

"The house is shut in by large gates from the street in front, and from our long windows at the back we have such a view as seldom delights the eye of man. Ernest and I stood long on the balcony admiring the superb sight. The valley just below spanned by the high viaduct, the opposite green hill covered with red-roofed villas, and just now perfectly white with the blossoms of spring.

"Two great windmills stand out against the distant sky, and beyond, a glimpse of the winding Seine which here just touches us, while below the magnificent view of Paris with its gilded domes, the buildings of the Trocadero, and great gates of the 'Champ de Mars,' spread far before us.

"The forest of Meudon is quite celebrated, and the château, built by the Grand Dauphin, is approached by a fine avenue of lime trees, while the whole town is embowered in every description of verdure, and standing so high must be healthy in the extreme. . . . Well, all our things arrived in safety and we have begun to settle. Now if Lu could only come and spend six months in this lovely place with us, with its pretty lanes, old ruined bits and quiet air, she would never want to return to America. So, dear Lu, do get well and sail for sunny France and I will make you so happy and comfortable! We can have such nice long days together with Ernest to take you to theatres, or anywhere you like.

"Imagine such a delightful year, for I am sure our future is a happy and secure one. . . . I feel as if I were living in somebody's else romance for I cannot believe it is mine. . . . Not a wish seems

ungratified except that Louisa is not well enough
to come and see and enjoy my good fortune with
me.

"Both Ernest and I feel that winter is not the
time for her to try Meudon, but we will try to
make her comfortable and by spring it will be
enchanting and she will have a delightful summer
with us. She must not think my own happiness
has made me unmindful of her, for it only draws
us nearer. But I have laid out my future life and
hope not to swerve from my purpose. I do not
mean to be hindered by envious people, or anything to divert me from accomplishing my dream.

"For myself this simple artistic life is so charming, that America seems death to all aspirations
or hope of work. I think I must have changed,
myself, for no one could enjoy more this quiet life,
with the sun and the birds, open windows and warm
breezes. Meudon seems a Paradise. With Ernest,
and pictures, I should not care if I never saw
a friend or acquaintance again. It is the perfection
of living; the wife so free from household cares,
so busy, and so happy. I never mean to have a
house, or many belongings, but lead the delightfully free life I do now with no society to bother
me, and nothing to prevent my carrying out my
aims and in succeeding in something before I

die. . . . I shall never regret my act for no possible amount of fame, glory, wealth or success could have brought me the happiness and real content of my married life."

The coming of letters from home which vividly recalled the recent bereavement, made May feel that she had hardly a right to her present happiness and she writes:

"Your letters seem almost a reproach to me for being able to forget that dear Marmee has gone from us even during this most happy time of my life.

"I think how she married for love and struggled with poverty and all possible difficulties and came out gloriously at last, all the stronger and happier for so mastering circumstances, and this gives me courage, hoping her example will be always a safe guide for me. In my case it will be easier to be brave, because Ernest is a practical, thrifty business man; he is young, ambitious, with real faculty instead of an impractical philosopher."

CHAPTER XII

May's Romance

MAY'S letters continue to describe the charm of her little home and the gradual acquisition of pieces of furniture, and effective draperies, which lent those artistic touches and warm tints that she loved so dearly. Her husband enjoyed picking up household treasures and often brought home in triumph purchases to adorn their rooms. After spending some time in their ground-floor apartment, they were able to secure one on the floor above, which gave them more room and greater conveniences. Of the arrangement there, May wrote enthusiastically, including every trifling detail, which she knew would be of interest to those at home:

"We have been very busy arranging our new apartment. The joke of the week has been Ernest coming home with an immense Louis XIV mirror. It has broad sloping sides in which are little mirrors framed in black and carved gilt. It is an elegant thing and we are both secretly convinced that it is too fine for our salon at present, though when we get our piano and my cabinet it will give all quite an air. I have in mind a rich old carved piece of furniture, a sort of secretary at which to write, and where we can lock up our papers. Our mirror now nearly fills one end of the oblong salon and reflects the whole room quite in Parisian style. Beneath it stands a great antique chair; at the other end is my tall Milo Venus against its crimson background."

She goes on to describe the arrangement of her rugs, pictures, and the interior of her little dining room, as well as the rest of her apartment, which she has beautified with a loving and artistic touch.

They entertain their first guests in September, when May's friends, the Pierces, drop in to see them on their return from Russia. May pictures their pleasure in inspecting her attractive little ménage and tells of her modest luncheon party:

"My table was inviting with its fine damask, my pretty silver and plenty of flowers and a green grape-leaf dish piled high with peaches, pears, and grapes. Salmon salad, Gervais cheese, cold tongue, nice cake and a *pâté douceurs* such as only the French can make, gave us a charming lunch, finished with wine. As Ernest ordered it all from Paris I felt sure it was 'comme il faut.'

"After we had enjoyed it heartily I proposed a

stroll to see the view, and we wandered up to the hill-top, and down the beautiful Avenue du Château, through the thick arch made by the overhanging trees. Through this vista we passed on to Sevres, entered the gate of the splendid Parc of St. Cloud and walking through the long shaded alleys reached the great terraces. Here we took our 'sirop' at one of the little tables, and rested awhile, and then took the boat homeward down the Seine. It was a lovely sail, seeing such pretty pictures through the many arched bridges, of wooded banks and picturesque groups resting among the trees. At *bas* Meudon they left me, going on themselves to Paris, after an affectionate farewell, and telling me what a truly ideal and charming day they had passed.

"And so had I, and after my labors were over, I sat down in my easy-chair to admire the effect of my pretty rooms. I had placed Marmee's shrine on my mantel and on one side my blue jar holding a long spray of morning-glories. Two buds had opened wide and laid themselves lovingly against the dear face, dropping gracefully the delicate vines around it. It was so beautiful, and Marmee seemed to have come to my party in spirit so that even amid my happiness I had to 'weep a little weep.'

MAY ALCOTT

"No matter how dear the husband, he can never be so precious as Marmee. I often in my mind picture her as she looked after riding, seated on the rustic bench under the big tree waiting for her cup of tea, the little crepe bonnet perhaps all on one side, but that handsome, pale face and soft hair so lovely to me. How happy we were driving together through Concord's green lanes, would I could do so once more."

The success of the Nierikers' first luncheon party proved an incentive to more entertaining, and on hearing that her friends the Lombards were in Paris, May invited them to luncheon, also suggesting that Frank Millet, the artist, should join the party. The latter was then making his headquarters in Paris, where he had served as a member of the Fine Arts Jury at the Exposition; he had seen May's work and praised it very highly, declaring that she would never have any difficulty in finding a market for it. Before this time, he had been called from his art work to the post of war correspondent for the *London Standard*, in the Russo-Turkish War, where he had faced many dangers and privations, and had gained a wide reputation with his pen, persisting in his work when less courageous correspondents had returned

to England. As one recalls the tragic close of his
brilliant career on the ill-fated S.S. *Titanic*, one
rests assured that in that final terrible emergency
the old-time courageous spirit did not fail him.
Upon the summer day in question, Frank Millet's
plan to join the little luncheon party at Meudon
failed to materialize. The day arrived sunny and
fine, and all the preparations had been made to
receive the guests from Paris, after which May and
her husband walked to the station to meet the
incoming train, which shortly arrived but without
the expected visitors. What had arisen to prevent
their coming is not chronicled in the remaining
letters, as May merely reports that she and her
husband ate their nice luncheon by themselves,
and vowed to plan no more parties for a long time
to come, adding:

"We took a charming walk to a fine old church
and priory, which I enjoyed very much, for this
old building stands very high on a hill overlook-
ing the sea with a winding lane leading to it,
between fresh green hedge-rows. The long wing
of the priory, half ruined with lovely bits of
architecture left standing in places, and just now
covered with vines of the brightest yellow, the
deep gorgeous gold lighted by the sun forming a

fine contrast to the cool gray of the old stone-work and the dark green of the luxuriant ivy which covers everything. Steep steps lead to the main entrance, for the church stands on a plateau in the midst of a flower garden, so brightly are the graves adorned everywhere with gay blossoms. It seems like anything rather than a graveyard."

She concludes:

"We wandered about the heights, in and out, and sat at last down to rest under the shadow of the Virgin and Child, which is so large it can be seen from all the country around. The view is beautiful of the sea, with Havre in the distance, distinguished from its neighbors by its forests of masts, and the white beacon at the end of the pier. We then sought the little café at the end of the lane , . . and so home again."

May had expressed the earnest hope that some memoir of her mother might be compiled, and in June, 1878, Mr. Alcott and Louisa made an attempt to carry out this project, dear to all their hearts, in memory of her who had been not only the inspiration and mainstay of the family, but had in both her letters and journals displayed a genuine literary quality that all felt should not be allowed to vanish without recognition.

In writing to May at this time her father said of this project:

"Louisa and I have set about compiling from your mother's Diaries and letters, a Memoir of her life, which Niles wishes to publish as soon as it is ready for the press. Your mother wrote much during some of the most eventful years of her life, and the Memoir may make a most edifying and instructive book. Sanborn will gladly assist us in its preparation.

"Louisa is improving daily, and for your sake dear May, I wish she may find you in your lovely nest before the cold weather comes, much as we shall be saddened by the change. And let me add that I am sad at the thought of your being so far from us, and that I may not see you again on this side the seas. But then your happiness consoles me and I try to be resigned to this separation."

The Memoir of Marmee to be compiled, and the visit to be made to May's new home, were two plans never to be realized. Both were dependent upon Louisa Alcott's state of health, and both were relinquished because she had not the strength, or the heart, to undertake them. As she read over those remarkable letters and journals, their contents seemed to her too personal and intimately bound up with family affairs for general publication, and she began the task of eliminating much, selecting only a small proportion of the precious memories set down. Following her mother's expressed wish, she destroyed all but a few fragments of the long personal history embodied in those faithfully penned diaries, though many of the letters still remain to testify to the gifted pen of their writer, the record of whose final years is here briefly presented. Louisa Alcott could ply her pen with lightning speed when bent upon depicting the living, whom she could outline with vivid strokes, but when she touched upon those that had gone, she faltered and laid her pen aside. And so the Memoir was never done.

And the much longed-for visit to May, so eagerly anticipated, also failed to materialize despite May's often expressed wish, for Louisa's health was very frail and she dreaded to undertake the journey until she should have strength to enjoy the trip with something of her former zest. Afterwards, she keenly regretted that she had not gone to the new home, to share in person those happy memories of May's brief married life, which she was destined to know only from letters telling of its joys, and of the pretty little home which May so longed to show to her, and of which she had written:

"Lu must come and see how charming things are, for we could have such pleasant days together. Ernest is always ready for any fun, and she could have my big sleeping-room with its crimsoned curtained-bed and open fire-place. You can imagine what comfort I take in these snug quarters, — Our *femme de ménage* is a treasure and cooks us delicious little dinners, brings the water, cleans the rooms, runs errands and seems honest and respectable. This gives me all my time to myself.

"I paint and walk and write all day. At night Ernest comes home and puts on his grey palatot, and lies in the grass beside me while I sew in the garden after our late dinner. I feel like one in a happy dream selfishly enjoying my life without a thought beyond; Ernest, my pictures, my home, are all I desire. There is not a cloud as big as your hand in my sky."

That the family had questioned the wisdom of her sudden marriage to a young foreigner, several years her junior, who had his way to make, and of whom they knew nothing, is evident from May's reiteration of her complete satisfaction and perfect confidence in her husband's ability and devotion. There are no doubts in her mind as to their future. She knows that all will be well; her work is bound to prove more and more successful, her husband will win wealth and recognition, and years of untrammeled joy will be theirs. One reads with trepidation of her childlike faith in her lucky star; she is so sure that one already trembles at the thought that such perfect bliss is likely to be fleeting. It is all too good to be true, this vision of a human being who has grasped her heart's desire, and who declaims that it is hers to keep, and that from now on the path that she will tread shall be mapped out exactly to her taste. She writes:

"I mean to combine painting and family, and show that it is a possibility if *let alone*. But not if I am at the mercy of constant company, who have no real claim on me and my time, so let me have my own way and devote this year at least to carrying out my aims. In America this cannot be done, but foreign life is so simple and free, we can live for our own comfort not for company. I often wonder if I could step back into my old life and feel at home there, for I seem quite a different person from the woman who bade you good-bye so long ago, and you would find me greatly changed.

"To be a happy wife with a good husband to love and care for me, and then go on with my art.

This blessed lot is mine, and from my purpose I never intend to be diverted. . . . I am free to follow my profession, I have a strong arm to protect, a tender love to cherish me, and I have no fears for the future. Set your dear hearts at rest, for could you see me in my lovely home amid birds and blossoms, and know my happiness you would say 'May has decided wisely'."

In June, the approaching visit of her husband's mother and brother from their home in Baden was an event of supreme importance to May, who dreaded this ordeal. The guest room was prepared and duly decorated with flowers for Mme. Nieriker, and a dainty supper was awaiting the guests when they arrived late in the evening, to find the little home bright with candles and flowers, and the new daughter, and sister, arrayed in her best blue gown. The meeting gave satisfaction to all parties concerned, and May found the cultivated German mother-in-law affectionate and sympathetic, and the brother-in-law was at once captivated by the charm of his new sister. May's French, which was not very fluent, was taxed to the utmost, but they got on admirably, and the visit was prolonged for more than a fortnight, during which period the guests spent considerable time with May at the Paris Exposition, which was then going on.

Insisting that May must not stay so much at home, they planned many excursions, and theater parties, and she went with them to the picture exhibitions, which she later described, commenting on the admirable work of her fellow countrymen:

"Our American department held its own among the others, and this surprised me, as well as made me proud, for though small, it is a good collection showing the study of the Americans under the teaching of the French, for in painting the French stand alone.

"Henry Bacon has a head quite like a Murillo, rich and strong, and Bridgman's 'Burial of the Nile' stands in the place of honor. Porter's head of Maud Howe is also here, and very fine the draperies and accessories are. Miss Cassatt's 'Yellow Woman' is there; Dana's fine study by moonlight, two good Vedders, and splendid oil and water-colors by Gifford, and Tiffany of New York.

"But to us the *chef d'œuvre* of the exposition is Munkaczy's, whose pictures excel any other master, always strong, rich in color, subdued in tone, masterly in execution. The present picture is 'Milton and the Daughters,' and is full of sentiment and very fine. We stood long enjoying it."

MAY'S ROMANCE

A study of the picture galleries was followed by some visits to the shops and May writes:

"Our day proved a pleasant one, and we finished with a little shopping in the big shops of Paris, which much amused Mama. She and Max spend much time in the city seeing all its wonders, and come home with great papers of strawberries, cakes and nice things for the late dinner. Our *femme de ménage* does very well, and my visitors are very thoughtful, often dining in Paris to give me quiet days for painting.

"Mama often says, 'Stick to your art, May, and let Ernest take care of himself.' She believes in women having a career as well as men. I shall be sorry when they leave, as they will do in a few days, having been here nearly three weeks."

The autumn found the bride viewing with satisfaction her summer accomplishment and she records the amount of work completed:

"Since July I've painted oils and water colors, fourteen sketches. Having already seven studies on exhibition in Paris, two just finished for Lille, a panel in the Manchester gallery, two in London, and an order ready for America, I feel that I can rest."

MAY ALCOTT

The pleasant association with the new mother in no way obscures the vivid picture of Marmee, which rises so often that she also seems a part of this life in France. May writes on October 8, 1878, to those at home:

Mother's Birthday, Meudon.

This morning I adorned dear Marmee's picture with late morning-glories wreathing them with many tender thoughts. Through the day I was constantly with you, wondering if you were at Sleepy Hollow, and how you would get through this season of sad recollections.

I remember you wrote me how you dressed my picture with flowers and put it where she could see it in those last days. How long it seemed that no word came, and then her last little note of farewell that will always break my heart to think of.

Ernest knowing how badly I felt took me for a long walk straying through the pretty woods till night came on. The cool green seemed to rest my eyes and head, and thoughts of my happy present with this dear companion to love and care for me, brought at last comfort and rest to my heart. . . . Most of our courtship has been done since we were married, and Meudon has seen more tender scenes than London ever did.

MAY'S ROMANCE

Winter at Meudon holds an equal charm for the members of the placid little household and May writes of their quiet Christmas:

"Some people might have thought our Christmas not a very gay one, but we enjoyed it greatly. E. presented me with a fine scarlet Diary and I spent the morning writing in it, making a summary of the events of this year, artistic, matrimonial, joyful, sad, and domestic, all of which made a varied story.

"Later Ernest and I took a beautiful walk together in the snowy Bois, which looked very fine in its winter dress. As we reached the extreme height the sky was lovely rose and green lighted by the setting sun, and as we stood looking at the magnificent landscape before us, we thought it quite as striking as in Summer when the avenue of rich green leads the eye naturally to the fine vista at the end, for in all France these are arranged for effect, and whichever way one turns one is struck by the charm and beauty. . . . In the evening we sat before our open-fire which burns in a low grate in the chimney-corner, just large enough for two. There we light our study lamp and read, write or talk French, in a most cozy fashion. There will always be to me a touch of romance in everything European, which is the charm perhaps which has brought me here for the third time, and now anchored me. Father will rejoice that I now have begun a diary that I may place on record many things which my sisters may sometime like to read.

"And be sure that whatever in the future may happen I regret nothing and believe our marriage the best and happiest thing for both. If trouble or sickness come how much easier to bear it together."

So the year closes in contentment and without regrets, but with perhaps a faint foreshadowing of the approach of a permanent separation from her loved ones across seas.

In reply to the questions of those at home regarding the appearance of her husband May wrote:

"You ask me about Ernest's face and character, and I will try to give you some idea of both. He is slender with broad shoulders, a delicate hand, and very handsome aristocratic foot. He has a beautifully shaped head with a profusion of brown hair curling about the brow, and he parts it in the middle. Large hazel eyes, a handsome nose with proud nostrils and as beautiful a mouth as I ever saw, almost perfect in form with a firm, decided chin below. His throat is round and white as a woman's and he wears an open collar which is very becoming.

"I often think as he stands looking up from the garden what a good, attractive face it is, the expression so fine with a sort of uplifted look, tender and sweet. In London at that long boarding-house table among the thirty faces, his stood out alone, attractive from its force and character.

"His is a noble nature, gentle and affectionate, and very tender yet high spirited and manly. . . . Ernest is quiet and reserved much more mature than I am, loves good books and good men. He is full of music, enjoying it best alone, handling his bow with exquisite delicacy and taste. He is highly gifted, and I think his one mistake has been relinquishing music for business. . . . His only fault seems to be a hasty temper, but it soon blows over and he is ready to make any reparation in his power. His good qualities far outweigh his faults."

May's love of crimson draperies and bits of brilliant scarlet for decorative purposes is offset by her intense love of blue for her own wearing apparel. From childhood she continually voices her love of blue dresses, and in her letters there is a frequent reference to her choice of some *blue*

material, for negligée or party gown; it is her color
and she revels in it. Her books are decorated with
forget-me-nots, or violets, and her love for the
former flower is many times expressed; she writes,
in 1878, at the close of the season, of her purchase
of a dress trimmed with her favorite blue flowers:

"I went early to Paris this morning to buy a
new costume, and after looking in vain for the
right thing, at last going into the Grande Magazin
du Louvre, the first thing my eyes lighted on was
a gray pongee silk with some solid masses of
forget-me-nots in long strips for trimming, and a
little mantle. I instantly saw the whole toilette,
bonnet the same color, with bunches of the flowers,
sunshade lined with blue. It is to be princess style,
fitting as only a Paris dressmaker can fit one, and
the ensemble with mantle, embroidered flounce
and bands, little pelisse and sunshade, a most
perfect turnout, and in proper Parisian taste, beside, costing only $40.

"I will also add that my brown Paris-made suit
with a high hat turned up with velvet and trimmed
with ostrich feathers is a handsome stylish dress."

In blue or brown, and always with a dashing
ostrich plume waving above her red-gold hair, —
that was May Alcott.

Her sister's happiness brought Louisa the keenest satisfaction. She forgot her own longing for her sister's companionship in the joy of contemplating the crowning happiness of that fortunate life; it was as it should be. And at this period, she noted in her journal, "Happy letters from May, who is enjoying life as one can but once." Then with a sudden vision of her own lonely lot, she exclaims:

"How different our lives are just now. I so lonely, and sick; and she so happy and blest. She always had the cream of things, and deserved it. My time is yet to come somewhere else, when I am ready for it."

Louisa's continued ill health made her unwilling to risk a voyage across seas, though she longed to visit her sister and make the acquaintance of her new brother. By resting throughout the summer she hoped to be able to undertake the journey but as the time approached she dared not risk the voyage, writing in disappointment:

"Got nicely ready to go to May in September; but at the last moment gave it up, fearing to undo all the good this weary year of ease has done for me, and be a burden on her. A great disappointment; but I've learned to wait. I long to see her happy in her new home."

[287]

Another artistic triumph came to May in the spring of 1879, when the second of her canvases found a place in the Salon, an event that gave special satisfaction to her father, who wrote upon receipt of the good news:

"Yes, surely, my happy child, you are to be congratulated, and again and again, on your success at the Salon, and in your husband's affections. I read your letter, announcing the acceptance of your picture, with pride, and almost wished, instead of the new name, euphonious as this is, the honor had been conferred upon Miss May Alcott. But even dutiful daughters are honored when taking their husband's name without loss of loyalty to their birthright. You are a successful member of our House. I shall be content while you continue to honor it with your friendship and your art in the future."

Of her picture of a young negress which had won special commendation he says:

"Were your picture here now in this crisis of the Slave Exodus, I know not what new honors might await the artist on this side the Atlantic. The negress might rival even Mrs. Stowe's 'Uncle Tom,' and as his counterpart, might couple your

name with hers, and Louisa's, whom we are informed are the only women authors much known
on the continent. At any rate, I am happy in
learning of your content to remain in France, taking life in a rational and right spirit, nor do I
yield the hope of seeing you here and welcoming
you and yours to your old home and country."

About this time Louisa writes: "Happy letters
from May. Her hopes of a little son, or daughter
in the autumn, give us new plans to talk over.
I *must* be well enough to go to her then."

In the late spring she speaks of the prospect of
renting Orchard House:

"It is forlorn standing empty. I never go by
without looking up at Marmee's window, where the
dear face used to be, and May's, with the picturesque vines around it. No golden-haired blue-
gowned Diana ever appears now; she sits happily
sewing baby-clothes in Paris. Enjoyed fitting out
a box of dainty things to send her. Even lonely
old spinsters take an interest in babies."

Two months before the birth of May's daughter
her father wrote, enclosing a present in the form
of the first money received from Orchard House,
which had been rented to Mr. Harris:

"Please accept from your father the first rent money yet received for the Orchard House since we left it nearly two years ago. It is but a trifle but it takes to you not a little affection, for yourself, and may I not add, for the *Little one*, the pledge of your love for the father, whom you have chosen for your friend and companion in your future sojourns! May every blessing await you and yours.

"You will wish to have a word along with this little token about the Orchard House itself. It is not unlikely that the estate may be purchased and dedicated to a "permanent school of Philosophy", and possibly I myself may occupy it. This is among the possibilities of the future."

After describing a meeting at Andover where he had addressed six hundred students and received quite an ovation, he concludes, "These latter years are bestowing honors and rewards for the indifference of former ones."

May's dreams and those of her father were coming true, but one may question, whether it was the hand of time bestowing these rewards, or that of the devoted daughter and sister, whose pen had been plied tirelessly in order that they might dream true.

MAY'S ROMANCE

In September, 1879, May sent home some letters describing "An Artist's Holiday", which her sister had printed; she also arranged for the publication of May's little book, written to furnish information to art students abroad. Of this work Louisa writes, "Very useful and well done."

In October, she again records her sad disappointment at not starting for Europe:

"Father goes west. I mourn because all say I must not go to May; not safe; and I cannot add to Mama Nieriker's cares at this time by another invalid, as the voyage would upset me, I am so seasick.

"Give up my hope and long-cherished plan with grief. May sadly disappointed. I know I shall wish I had gone; it is my luck."

And now May's star, so long in the ascendant, began to glimmer faintly, for the joyful event so long anticipated was bringing with it gathering clouds soon to obscure its brightness.

CHAPTER XIII

Farewell and Hail

On the eighth of November, 1879, little Louisa May Nieriker arrived in Paris. There was great rejoicing in the Alcott family, and especially in the heart of Louisa, at the thought of her little namesake. Yet with the joy was mingled some anxiety for May in that far distant city with none of her own family about her. Louisa felt that she should have been there to watch and to assist in any possible emergency which might arise.

At first all promised well and she endeavored to banish dark forebodings, though she still cherished much regret at being far away from the small namesake and her mother, exclaiming:

"Nice little lass, and May very happy. Ah, if I had only been there! Too much happiness for me. Two years since Marmee went. How she would have enjoyed the little grand-daughter, and all May's romance! Perhaps she does."

Letters from their kind friend Miss Plummer brought news of May's failure to rally as she should. The family were filled with keen anxiety and on Louisa's forty-seventh birthday, November 29, she wrote:

"May not doing well. The weight on my heart is not all imagination. She was too happy to have it last, and I fear the end is coming. Hope it is my nerves; but this peculiar feeling has never misled me before."

Letters from Paris brought varying reports, some hopeful and others despairing, and on December 8, Louisa Alcott wrote of her namesake:

"Little Lu, one month old. Small but lively. Oh, if I could only be there to see and help. This is a penance for all my sins. Such tugging at my heart to be by poor May, alone, so far away. The Nierikers are devoted, and all is done that can be; but not one of her 'very own' is there."

But all regrets were useless, and she consoled herself with the thought that her coming to May's household in her uncertain health might have brought only added anxiety to all. Yet, on the other hand, she knew that her own mental poise and power of self-control would have no doubt enabled her to surmount her own ills and to command the situation. The Nierikers were untiring in their devotion, but had she been there, her presence would have meant much to her sister, who had always depended on her in time of need. And then, in the emergency of May's fast-failing strength, who can say that Louisa's prompt and decisive methods might not have saved the day? At the beginning of unfavorable symptoms, she would assuredly have summoned to her sister's bedside the best of Paris experts, yet none can say that the result would have been different.

On the 29th of December May died, after three weeks of fever and stupor, and Louisa wrote of the coming of their dear friend, Ralph Waldo Emerson, to break the news to her.

"A dark day for us. A telegram from Ernest to Mr. Emerson tells us 'May is dead.' Anna was gone to Boston; Father to the post-office anxious for letters overdue. I was alone when Mr. Emerson came. Ernest sent to him, knowing I was feeble, and hoping Mr. E. would soften the blow. I found him looking at May's portrait, pale and tearful, with the paper in his hand. 'My child, I wish I could prepare you; but alas, alas!!' There his voice failed, and he gave me the telegram.

"I was not surprised, and read the hard words as if I knew them all before. 'I am prepared,' I said, and thanked him. He was much moved and very tender. I shall remember gratefully the look, the grasp, the tears, he gave me; and I am sure that hard moment was made bearable by the presence of our best and tenderest friend. He went to find Father but missed him, and I had to tell both him and Anna when they came. A very bitter sorrow to us all. . . . 'Two years of perfect happiness,' May called these married years, and said, 'If I die when baby comes don't mourn, for I have had as much happiness in this short time as many in twenty years.' She wished me to have her baby and her pictures. A very precious legacy. Rich payment for the little I could do for her. I see now why I lived, to care for May's child and not to leave Anna alone."

Mr. Alcott's sorrow found an outlet in the production of a poem commemorating this daughter of whom he had been so proud, and his journal for 1880 opens with his poem "Love's Morrow", written immediately after receiving the news of May's death. This poem ends with the stanzas:

> Transported May!
> Thou could'st not stay,
> Who gave took thee away.
> Come, child, and whisper peace to me;
> Say must I wait, or come to thee?
> I list to hear
> Thy message clear.

"Cease, cease, more grief to borrow,"
Last night I heard her say;
"For sorrow has no morrow,
'T is born of yesterday."
Translated thou must be,
My cloudless daylight see,
And bathe, as I, in fairest morrows endlessly.

The father records that this expression of his sorrow and hope brought him much consolation; he carried the verses over to his friend, Frank Sanborn, and after reading them to him, he noted in his journal, "This may yield me sleep and repose again. But Anna and Louisa! They must grieve long."

This was indeed true. But Louisa also took up her pen and on the selfsame night produced her truly beautiful memorial poem, "Our Madonna."

Letters followed from the grief-stricken husband, telling the sad story. May was unconscious during the last weeks, and seemed not to suffer, but from time to time she spoke of getting ready for her sister Louisa, and asked if she had come?

She had felt a foreboding of what was in store for her, and had left all in readiness in case of her going. Trunks were packed with articles to be sent home. Her journal was carefully written up, and she had chosen the cemetery where she wished to rest in case she did not survive. She had also exacted the promise that in the event of her death her child should be sent back to Louisa, to receive the devoted care that she knew would be given by her sister.

After the receipt of the sad news Louisa wrote to her aunt Mrs. Bond:

"Gone, to begin the new year with mother, in a world where I hope there is no grief like this. Gone just when she seemed safest and happiest, after nearly two years of such love and sweet satisfaction that she wrote us: 'If I die when baby comes, remember I have been so unspeakably happy for a year that I ought to be content.' And it is all over. The good mother and sister have done everything in the most devoted way. We can never repay them. My May gave me her little Lulu, and in the spring I hope to get my sweet legacy. Meantime the dear grandma takes her to a home full of loving friends and she is safe. I will write more when we know, but the cruel sea divides us and we must wait."

The bereaved father derived much consolation from the sympathy of his old friends who had loved May, to whose memory he paid special tribute by carrying his verses about and reading them to various individuals and sorrowful groups.

MAY ALCOTT

The warm sympathy of the Concord friends is chronicled in his journal:

"Neighbors kindly call and speak tender words; May had served the young people particularly, and left them indebted for her art-school instruction. Many letters of sympathy have come to me from friends elsewhere. Though absent during these last two years, she is remembered with affectionate regard, and her decease sincerely mourned. Ah, how death humanizes and fraternizes the living, as it would bind them in closer and enduring union here and hereafter."

Mr. Alcott notes the receipt of the first letters describing the funeral services:

"Accounts of the last sad ceremonies reach us in a letter from a friend of May's, who saw her frequently during her last illness and was present at her burial. Of the particulars it is most pleasing to recall the obeisances of the passers-by as the little cortege slowly wound its way through the streets. And when the pall was removed the casket was 'white.' 'Ah, my May, thou could'st not have chosen an emblem more befitting thyself and the art thou loved. White, spotless, be thy memory."

FAREWELL AND HAIL

This month's record closes with a brief appreciation from the father's pen, headed, "May":

"Her temperament was elastic, susceptible; she had a lively fancy, a clear understanding. She possessed fine social qualities and her temper was imperturbable. She had a fine sense of honor and decorum. Independence was a marked trait. Her manners were positive and perpetual. She held her fortunes in her hand, and failure was a word unknown in her vocabulary of effort. Her figure was graceful, she was taller than the average of her sex.

"When last seen by me, she was standing on the steamer's deck, and waved her handkerchief till lost in the distance. Her active career has now closed in the height of her happiness and fame, and she has passed into a future of fuller opportunities and holier engagements. Yes, and rejoices now with those who have gone from our sight before."

Louisa Alcott had written at the opening of the year 1880:

"A sad day mourning for May. Of all the trials of my life, I never felt any so keenly as this; perhaps because I am so feeble in health that I cannot bear it well. It seems so hard to break up that happy little home, and take May, just when life was richest, and leave me who had done my task and could well be spared."

But Louisa's task was not yet complete, as those eight remaining years proved conclusively.

After a renewed period of sadness, which followed the coming across seas of a trunk full of mementoes, — May's pictures, her clothes, and many little personal belongings, that wakened so vividly the happy memories of other days, — thoughts of the coming of May's child awoke new hope and expectation. Plans were made for the reception of the baby in the early autumn, and an experienced woman was sent abroad to take charge of the child, and to accompany the young Aunt Sophie, who was to take the journey with her.

About this time, Louisa wrote to a member of her family:

"May left me her little daughter for my own; and if she comes over soon, I shall be too busy singing lullabies to one child to write tales for others, or go anywhere, even to see my kind friends. A sweeter little romance has just ended in Paris than any I can ever make; and the sad facts of life leave me no heart for cheerful fiction."

Yet her gifted pen was destined to produce many
more tales of hope and cheer to delight thousands
of young readers. And with the coming of the
autumn, the bereaved sister found a new spirit of
hope and joy springing up in her heart, as she
prepared for the arrival of May's baby, writing of
the event:

"Got things ready for my baby, warm wrapper,
and all the dear can need on her long journey.
On the 21st, saw Mrs. Giles off; the last time I
went it was to see May go. She was sober and
sad, not gay as before; seemed to feel it might be a
longer voyage than we knew. The last view I had
of her was standing alone, in the long blue cloak,
waving her hand to us, smiling with wet eyes till
out of sight. How little we dreamed what an
experience of love, joy, pain, and death she was
going to!"

A few days later she notes that all is in readiness
for the arrival of little Lulu, declaring: "Make a
cozy nursery for the darling, and say my prayers
over the little white crib that waits for her."

On September 18, 1880, she went to Boston to
be on hand for the incoming steamer due to arrive
the following day; and she has pictured the exciting moment of the child's arrival:

[301]

"As I waited on the wharf while the people came off the ship, I saw several babies, and wondered each time if that was mine. At last the captain appeared, and in his arms a little yellow-haired thing in white, with its hat half off as it looked about with lively blue eyes and babbled prettily. I held out my arms to Lulu, only being able to say her name. She looked at me for a moment, then came to me saying 'Marmar' in a wistful way, and resting close as if she had found her own people and home at last, as she had, thank Heaven! . . . The little princess was received with tears and smiles, and being washed and fed went quietly to sleep in her new bed, while we brooded over her and were never tired of looking at the little face of 'May's baby.'

"My heart is full of pride and joy, and the touch of the dear little hands seems to take away the bitterness of grief. I often go at night to see if she is really *here*, and the sight of the little head is like sunshine to me. Father adores her, and she loves to sit in his strong arms. They make a pretty picture as he walks in the garden with her to 'see birdies.' Anna tends her, as she did May, who was her baby once, being ten years younger, and we all find life easier to live now the baby has come."

FAREWELL AND HAIL

Mr. Alcott pens his own impression of the new-comer:

"Our little Louisa May Nieriker is brought safely, and looks smilingly upon us, of her kindred, on this side the seas. A bright, blue-eyed Babe, and motherless now. I know not whether my emotion on beholding her first eager glance, partook more of surprise, of sadness, or of joy, as I recalled the accident of her birth, and prospects of her future, yet all unknown to me. She is here now at last, and with her mother's kindred to be kindly cared for during her tender infancy.

"Anna and Louisa have now a sweet charge to vary their cares and recreations. They will cherish the little one lovingly as the surviving token of their departed sister. Our house now no stranger to the attraction of a Babe. . . .

"Thanks, renewed thanks, to our Father, for all these prospects and past blessings many and dear."

The grandfather's journal at this time presents numerous verses, dedicated to the "Babe", and he writes of the interest awakened in the town by her coming:

"Many of our neighbors have called to see our little lady bright. And today Mrs. Emerson walks hither to pay her respects. A babe is the ornament of the house, and of the household in a Christian civilization."

Playing mother to the child May had left her brought a new restfulness to Louisa Alcott's tired brain, and did much to restore the old-time cheerfulness, despite the increased responsibility. The little namesake needed her constant thought, but she was happy in the new rôle of "Marmar", and she delighted to find May's child growing to be more and more like her mother. She wrote regarding her:

"I wish you could see the pretty creature, who already shows many of her mother's traits and tastes. Her love of pictures is a passion, but she will not look at the gay ones most babies enjoy. She chooses the delicate, well-drawn, and painted figures of Caldecott and Miss Greenaway. Over these she broods with rapture, pointing her little fingers at the cows or cats, and kissing the children, with funny prattlings to these dumb playmates. She is a fine, tall girl, full of energy, intelligence and health; blonde and blue-eyed like her mother, but with her father's features. Louisa May bids fair to be a noble woman, and I hope I may live to see May's child as brave, and bright, and talented as she was, and much happier in her fate."[1]

In the autumn of 1885, Miss Alcott moved to a furnished house at Number 10 Louisburg Square, Boston, and there, despite ill health, prepared three volumes of her stories for publication, entitled, "Lulu's Library." She also completed "Jo's Boys", the sequel to "Little Men", for which the public had long been clamoring. In the preface to this volume she touches upon her inability to continue the character of "Amy", accounting for this seeming neglect in the following words:

"Since the original died, it has been impossible for me to write of her, as when she was here to suggest, criticise, and laugh over her namesake. The same excuse applies to *Marmee*. But the folded leaves are not blank to those who knew and loved them, and can find memorials of them in whatever is cheerful, true, or helpful in these pages."

Louisa's gift to May, — how can one measure it! Such gifts can never be computed; gifts that embrace a lifetime of love and sympathy and rare

[1] After Louisa Alcott's death, Louisa May Nieriker made her home with her father in Europe; she married Ernst Rasim in 1903, and is now a widow with one daughter, Ernestine, born 1904.

companionship. At the cost of much sacrifice, Louisa helped May to realize her desires and ambitions, bearing additional burdens in order that she might be free to carry on her work abroad; yet with this sacrifice of time and strength there came to her a happiness and satisfaction that she could never have attained elsewhere. May was in many ways the instrument of joy in her famous sister's life, and her last gift of a child that Louisa could call her own came as the final payment for all the benefits received.

May's little daughter came back to be the joy and consolation of the lonely woman's last years, and none may estimate the value of this loving association that ended only with Louisa Alcott's death.

One loves to cherish the remembrance of the happy hours spent with the little namesake, and may well treasure the picture drawn by the author of "Little Women", on the first birthday of May's daughter:

"November 8, Lulu's birthday. One year old. Her gifts were set out on a table for her to see when she came down in the afternoon, — a little cake with *one* candle, a rose-crown for the queen, a silver mug, dolly, picture-books, gay ball, toys, flowers, and many kisses. She sat smiling at her treasures just beneath her mother's picture. Suddenly, attracted by the sunshine on the face of the portrait, which she knows is 'Marmar', she held up a white rose to it, calling 'Mum, Mum', and smiling."

And so Louisa places the "May Queen's" crown on the brow of May's tiny daughter, her own child now, who held in her uplifted hand a rose before her mother's shrine. And all knew that May would have had it so; May who loved romance, and whose happy life held no regrets.

May's dream that she should achieve lasting fame with brush and pencil was never to be realized, for it is not by her own pictures that she is destined to be remembered, but by that more enduring portrait painted by her sister, who created "Amy" for the delight of millions of young readers. This picture, so truthfully transcribed, remains among the permanent portraits in the gallery of our literature, where "Amy, the artist" will be remembered, not for her admirable work, but for her vivid self as portrayed by Louisa Alcott's pen.

MAY ALCOTT

OUR MADONNA

(Written by Louisa Alcott on receipt of the news of May's death, Jan., 1880)

A child, her wayward pencil drew
On margins of her book
Garlands of flowers, dancing elves,
Bird, butterfly and brook.
Lessons undone, and play forgot
Seeking with hand and heart
The teacher whom she learned to love
Before she knew 't was Art.

A maiden, full of lofty dreams,
Slender and fair and tall
As were the goddesses she traced
Upon her chamber wall.
Still laboring with brush and tool,
Still seeking everywhere
Ideal beauty, grace and strength
In the "divine despair."

A woman, sailing forth alone,
Ambitious, brave, elate,
To mould life with a dauntless will,
To seek and conquer fate.
Rich colors on her palette glowed
Patience bloomed into power;
Endeavor earned its just reward,
Art had its happy hour.

A wife, low sitting at his feet
To paint with tender skill
The hero of her early dreams,
Artist, but woman still.
Glad now to shut the world away,
Forgetting even Rome;
Content to be the household saint
Shrined in a peaceful home.

FAREWELL AND HAIL

A mother, folding in her arms
The sweet, supreme success;
Giving a life to win a life,
Dying that she might bless.
Grateful for joy unspeakable,
In that brief, blissful past;
The picture of a baby face
Her loveliest and last.

Death the stern sculptor, with a touch
No earthly power can stay,
Changes to marble in an hour
The beautiful, pale clay.
But Love the mighty master comes
Mixing his tints with tears,
Paints an immortal form to shine
Undimmed by coming years.

A fair Madonna, golden-haired,
Whose soft eyes seem to brood
Upon the child whose little hand
Crowns her with motherhood.
Sainted by death, yet bound to earth
By its most tender ties,
For life has yielded up to her
Its sacred mysteries.

So live, dear soul, serene and safe,
Throned as in Raphael's skies,
Type of the love, the faith, the grief
Whose pathos never dies.
Divine or human still the same
To touch and lift the heart:
Earth's sacrifice to Heaven's fame,
And Nature's truest Art.

INDEX

INDEX

INDEX

INDEX

"Little Raphael," 3, 31.

"Little Women," the writing and completion of, 67–68; publication of, 69.

Lombard, Fanny, 200.

Lombard, George, 228, 229.

London, at Brompton Road in, 100; studies under Rowbotham in, 100; 103–123; Kensington Museum, 106; Westminster Abbey, 107; the Shah of Persia in, 111–114; with Mrs. Moulton in, 159; plans to continue work in, 240; 243–248; learns of her mother's death, 249; 250–257; meets Ernest Nieriker in, 257–263.

Lovejoy, Mr., 30.

Low, Will H., 196–197, 212, 214, 217; letter from, 221–223.

"Lulu's Library," completion of, 305.

Luminais, Evariste Vital, 139.

Manet, Edouard, 195.

Manning, Abby, 235.

Manning, Misses, 206.

Marston, Philip Bourke, 157, 159.

Martin, Homer, 227.

Martineau, Harriet, 230.

May, Abigail. See Alcott, Mrs. Amos Bronson.

May, Samuel J., Mrs. Alcott's brother, 50, 52, 236.

Meissonier, Jean Louis Ernest, 183.

Mill, John Stuart, 62.

Millet, Frank, invited to May's luncheon, 272; death of, 273.

Millet, Jean François, at Barbizon, 203–204; 213–214.

Morris, William, 159.

Moss, Mr., 145, 146, 194, 199.

Moulton, Louise Chandler, and a biographical sketch of Louisa Alcott, 156; association with the poet Philip Bourke Marston, 157–159.

Müller, Carl, 139, 163–165, 170, 179, 180–181.

Munkaczy, Mihaly, 280.

Munroe, William, of Concord, death of, 228.

Murdock, Mr., 166.

National Academy of Design, 227.

Nieriker, Ernest, acquaintance with May Alcott, 257, 258; engagement of, 260; marriage of, 262; May's description of, 284–285.

Nieriker, Louisa May, birth of, 292; arrival in this country, 301–302; first birthday of, 306–307.

Niles, Thomas, of Roberts Brothers, 63.

"Old-Fashioned Girl, An", 64; publication of, 71.

Orchard House, the purchase of, in 1857, 45; the remodeling of, 48–49.

Osbourne, Mrs., May's friend, 219, 221.

Osbourne, Isobel. See Field, Mrs. Salisbury.

"Our Madonna," by Louisa Alcott, 308–309.

Paris, locates in, for art study, 138; studies in, under Monsieur Krug, 138; recommends, for the study of art, 139; daily life in, 141–143; "Prix de Rome," held in, 234–235; studio of the famous Couture in, 173–176; and the Salon of 1877, 191–193.

Parker, Theodore, 43.

Peckham, the Misses, May's roommates in Paris, 138, 141.

Peckham, Rose, paints portrait of May Alcott, 178; portraits of, refused for Salon, 193.

Pierce, Mr., 153.

Plummer, Miss, 292.

[314]

INDEX

Porter, Mr., 280.

Portraits, charcoal, by May, 35.

Powers, Hiram, 96.

Pratt, John, betrothal to Anna Alcott, 47; marriage, 50; death of, 99; 137.

Pratt, Mrs. John, journal of, quoted, 7, 8, 9, 11, 12, 13; letter from mother, 13–14; letter from Louisa, 39–40; engagement of, 47; marriage of, 50; letters from May, 74–75; serious illness of, 103.

"Prix de Rome," of 1877, 234–235.

Ramsey, Milne, 152, 200, 206.

Rimmer, Doctor William, 57.

Rodin, Auguste, his "Man of the Bronze Age," 195.

Rossetti, Dante Gabriel, 159.

Rousseau, Théodore, 204, 214.

Ruskin, John, praises May Alcott's work, 109.

Saint-Gaudens, Augustus, 197, 226

Salon, the, of 1877, 191–205; May exhibits painting in, 192, 193.

Sanborn, Frank, 171, 173.

Shaw, Quincy A., 204.

Shirlaw, Walter, 226.

South Kensington Museum, description of, 106.

Stevenson, Robert Louis, 196; at Grez, 215.

Still-Life, study in, in Salon of 1877, 192, 193; 208, 245–246.

Stowe, Harriet Beecher, 288.

Swinburne, Algernon Charles, 159.

Taylor, Mr. and Mrs. Peter, 62.

"Temple School," the, in Boston, 10.

Thiers, Louis Adolphe, 200.

Thoreau, Henry, 240.

Thoreau, Sophia, death of, 137; 240.

"Transcendental Wild Oats," 15.

Troyon, Constant, 183, 204.

Tuckerman, Salisbury, 106.

Turner, J. W. M., May's admiration for paintings by, 34, 35, 108, 109, 110; danger of the loss of his pictures, 110–111.

Vedder, Elihu, 280.

Warren, Lena, 81, 83, 84.

"Wayside, The," the later name for "Hillside," 20.

Webster, Albert, 154.

Wendt, Charles, 171, 172.

Westminster Abbey, privilege of sketching in, 107.

Whistler, James McNeill, 227.

Whitman, Alfred, a friend of the Alcotts, 61–62.

Wisinewski, Ladislas, the original of Laurie in "Little Women," 61, 167, 168.

Wister, Mrs. Owen, 145.

"Work," the writing of, by Louisa, 103.

9 781429 093125